KV-210-782

This book is to be returned on or before the
date stamped below. 27

Markets, Managers and Theory in Education

John Halliday

 The Falmer Press

(A member of the Taylor & Francis Group)
London • New York • Philadelphia

UK   The Falmer Press, Rankine Road, Basingstoke, Hampshire, RG 24 0PR

USA   The Falmer Press, Taylor & Francis Inc., 1900 Frost Road, Suite 101, Bristol, PA 19007

© J. Halliday 1990

First published 1990

British Library Cataloguing in Publication Data
Halliday, John
Markets, managers and theory in education.
1. Philosophy of education
I. Title
370.1

ISBN 1–85000–877–9
ISBN 1–85000–878–7 pbk

Library of Congress Cataloging-in-Publication Data
Halliday, John, 1950–
    Markets, managers, and theory in education/John Halliday.
        p.   cm.
    Includes bibliographical references and index.
    ISBN 1–85000–877–9 : —ISBN 1–85000–878–7 (pbk.)
    1. Education—Philosophy.   2. Education—Aims and
objectives.   3. Labor supply—Effect of education on.
4. Curriculum planning.   5. Education and state.   I. Title.
LB880.H28M37   1990
370′.1—dc20   90–41513
                                                         CIP

Jacket design by Caroline Archer
Typeset in 11/13 pts Bembo
by Graphicraft Typesetters Ltd., Hong Kong

Printed in Great Britain by Burgess Science Press, Basingstoke
on paper which has a specified pH value on final paper
manufacture of not less than 7.5 and is therefore 'acid free'.

Contents

Contents

Preface

I imagine that few people would dispute the claim that the words 'markets' and 'managers' are increasingly used in the context of debate about educational policy. However, I imagine that many people would dispute the claim that this increasing use is desirable. This book is an attempt: to explain the philosophical underpinnings of the educational uses of terms that share a 'family resemblance' with 'markets' and 'managers'; to criticize these underpinnings; to argue for an alternative to them; and to explain the educational implications of this alternative. Thus the book is an indirect attack on the enthusiastic incorporation of the terms 'markets' and 'managers' within educational theory and practice.

While the book is intended to be an academic monograph that is located within the general area of philosophy of education and the specific area of epistemology, it may also be of use to those who have a philosophical interest in the question of educational theory, but little existing philosophical background. Thus it may serve as an introduction to much recent work in the philosophy of education that is concerned with the logic of the relationship between educational theory and practice. Such an introduction may be of interest to educational theorists of an empirical persuasion, to students of the philosophy of education and to those people who have a general interest in education.

Teachers and others professionally concerned with education may be located in the latter category. These people may be interested in theories that underpin three currently popular ideas: vocationalism is the idea that the central purpose of education is to prepare people for work; managerialism is the idea that this preparation can be managed by those not intimately concerned with the practice of teaching; and consumerism is the idea that education should be led by the demands of the 'market'. While the book is most likely to interest those who are generally critical of the present dominance of these three ideas in curriculum theory and practice, it should also provoke some interest from the promoters of these ideas.

The initial reaction of some teachers to a philosophical analysis of this kind may be to feel that the limited time that they have available for reflection is increasingly spent perusing the latest guidelines for teaching, criteria for assessment, reports of working parties and so on. These teachers may complain that the thrust of present educational policy is directed towards the improvement of the instrumental activity of achieving curricular objectives that are set for them by others. They may recognize that this instrumentalism is antithetical to reflection upon the purpose of the activities in which they are engaged. Yet I argue that the dominance of instrumentalism within educational policy coheres with certain philosophical theories that are mistaken. It follows from this argument that philosophical reflection may help to explain the nature of a practical predicament. While it is not possible to claim that a set of philosophical theories is a cause of the shortage of time that teachers have for reflection, I believe that it is possible to claim that different philosophical theories and teaching practices cohere to differing degrees. In this book I argue for a set of theories and practices that allow time for philosophical reflection.

Throughout the book I have taken care to explain technical terms as they are introduced and I have included extensive footnotes where I think that a longer explanation might help the reader who is not yet 'on the inside' of philosophical terms and arguments. I also begin each chapter with a summary that may help both the philosophically sophisticated reader who might wish to skip the detail of certain arguments — and others who prefer to grasp the central thrust of an argument before getting involved in the detail.

As a central argument of the book is directed against empiricist epistemology, some readers may find it helpful to note at the outset that an empiricist epistemology is simply the theory of knowledge that we come to know things through experience. It may also be worth noting that one of the reasons for the popularity of this epistemology or theory of knowledge is that natural science is widely believed both to be the most successful way of getting knowledge and to be primarily concerned with finding things out through 'experience'.

In the last thirty years or so, many attempts to elucidate the logic of educational theory and its relation to practice have been informed by the idea that educational theory should guide rational practice by providing knowledge whose 'objectivity' is founded on the notion of 'experience'. Consequently, many curricular and managerial practices in education are also informed by this idea. I argue, however, that some of these practices have undesirable educational implications and that the idea that informs them is underpinned by an empiricist epistemology that has been widely criticized on philosophical grounds.

This book offers the beginnings of an alternative elucidation of the logical links between educational theory and practice based on a notion of hermeneutics derived from the work of H.G. Gadamer, T.S. Kuhn, R. Rorty and C. Taylor. It is argued that educational, natural scientific and other types of theory develop holistically within a theoretical network rather than individually against the foundations of 'experience' and that the linguistic practices of theoretical communities share a set of 'family resemblances' in discourse that makes it possible for theorists to interpret what each of them is doing and in this way to come to prefer some theories over others.

A discussion of 'critical theory' serves to illustrate the basis on which some interpretations are to be preferred over others and, from this discussion, it is proposed that educational theory should be seen as an interpretive practice. In order that such theory might be validated, some curricular and managerial changes within educational institutions are suggested and the book concludes with a discussion of the roles that the notions of vocationalism, managerialism and consumerism might play in a hermeneutic conception of educational theory.

As this book is based on my PhD thesis, I should like to thank Professor D.N. Aspin, formerly of King's College London, now of Monash University for his work as supervisor of the original research. I should also like to thank those friends, colleagues and members of my family who, in various ways, supported and encouraged me as I supplemented and restructured the original thesis.

John Halliday
July 1990

Introduction

During the past ten years or so, there seems to have been a constant supply of statements, policies and arguments that assert or purport to show that education in western capitalist democracies is in some sort of crisis and that this putative crisis is damaging both to individuals and to nations. For example, in North America, the publication of *A Nation at Risk*[1] led to a 'great debate' about the policies and theories that should inform the practices of those who worked within the education system. In Britain, the so-called 'Ruskin Speech'[2] by the then Prime Minister, James Callaghan, led to another 'great debate'. The role that the education system should play in promoting both economic prosperity and social cohesion has been central in both 'great debates'. Moreover in both America and Britain, Conservative governments seem to have been concerned primarily with the type of education that would secure economic growth.[3]

In Britain, this priority is most clearly seen in the rise of the Department of Employment's influence on the curriculum. It is claimed that in 1984–5 the Department of Employment spent over £2 billion[4] through the Manpower Services Commission (MSC) on special schemes designed to 'vocationalize' the curriculum. Since then, expenditure on these special schemes has increased considerably and on many occasions it has been argued on behalf of the MSC that the prime purpose of education should be to prepare people for work so that the nation's economic decline is arrested.[5] While it is not so easy to generalize about the vocationalism within American education, there is some evidence to suggest that something similar has happened.[6] Education appears to have been viewed primarily as a massive investment in the state's future prosperity — an investment that may be recouped in the form of increased productivity of the work force.

Common themes may be detected in debates about educational

priorities that have taken place within both countries: the liberal idea that a central purpose of education is to promote individual autonomy may be seen to have informed educational policy during much of the post-war era. It was believed by many commentators that such policy is not only morally justifiable but also instrumentally justifiable as the means to achieve greater social cohesion — it was expected that individuals would develop common frames of reference within which conflicting interests could be articulated and resolved. It was also expected that individuals would have an equal opportunity to gain the economic rewards that were on offer through a sort of open competition within the traditional liberal arts curriculum.

It is now widely accepted that this educational policy failed as a social policy. Existing inequalities were largely perpetuated and social cohesion was not promoted as common standards of evaluation did not evolve. Instead, there appears to have been something of a disjuncture between those who achieved material prosperity and security through their success within the liberal arts curriculum and those who did not. The disjuncture was all the greater because those who succeeded tended to value democratic citizenship and the means of resolving conflicts in discourse whereas those who failed had neither the means nor the common values to be able to resolve their disputes in this way. Instead these 'failures' (who were in the majority) looked to the certainty of maximizing material possessions as a neutral arbiter when deciding their priorities and values.

Conservative governments in both countries were able to utilize the preponderance of these materialistic values in the formulation of educational policies. Three important ideas were promoted: vocationalism is the idea that curricula should be designed to prepare people for particular occupations; managerialism is the idea that this preparation can be managed by those not intimately concerned with teaching; and consumerism is the idea that planning by the state is bound to fail and that individuals should be free to purchase their vocational preparation from a range of educational options or 'modules'. Thus education is promoted as a sort of service industry that should be consumer-led and managed according to principles that are taken from the worlds of industry and commerce. It is worth noting that many consumers still choose to enter something akin to the old liberal arts curriculum dominated by external examinations. It is also worth noting that many employers seem to favour this type of vocational preparation for their managers and better paid employees.[7]

It seems that a particular version of a liberal education failed as an instrument of social policy and was held by many supporters of

Conservative governments to have contributed to a decline in post-war economic prosperity. These supporters believed that the notion of the 'market' offered a much quicker, cheaper and fairer way of settling difficult issues of educational policy to the improvement of economic prosperity and equality of opportunity. On this view people could choose between the type of vocational education on offer on the basis of their desired occupation and the likely rewards that this occupation might bring.[8] However, as I and others argue, the 'market' is not such a neutral arbiter as its proponents might suggest. Instead the 'market' can be manipulated to secure a variety of objectives. The key factor in its adoption as a central feature in educational policy is that educational aims come to be formulated by an ever smaller group of people.[9] The majority is left to make a choice between various instruments for achieving those aims.

The implications of all this for traditional ideas of democratic citizenship are obvious and disturbing. The idea that a democratic consensus is achievable on issues that are heavily value-laden like the nature of educational policy is rejected in favour of the idea that democratic participation is little more than an expression of personal preference for a particular range of limited options that are presented in an attractive way. Such options are designed to achieve objectives that are set by and encapsulate the values of a minority. This rejection leaves liberal educational values in limbo. Not only is it supposed by many supporters of the 'new right' that the adoption of these values is a cause of previous economic failure and lack of opportunity for many people — but also the political agenda has shifted to such an extent that the appropriate criteria and contexts for evaluating liberal educational ideas are lived and articulated only within a small and perhaps decreasing number of people. The majority has been led to believe that democratic citizenship based on the liberal idea of promoting rational autonomy is both expensive and unfair. Even critics on the left of the political spectrum have suggested that the notion of democratic citizenship is simply a mask for the underlying set of power relations that dominate in a capitalist society.[10]

In such circumstances perhaps it is not surprising that critics of what we might call 'market-managerialism' should be somewhat despairing in their tone. One such critic concludes a recent article as follows:

> It is thus scarcely surprising that the idea of an educational science as a form of democratic moral discourse now lacks the social context necessary for its practical application.[11]

Perhaps the most trenchant criticism of 'market-managerialism' has emanated from Marxist and neo-Marxist writers. These writers might agree with the following theory:

> Successful capitalist economies require a large number of people prepared and willing to fill any employment vacancies that might arise. In this way the price of labour remains low and those who already control the means of production continue to do so. The state education system is an important instrument for securing low-price labour. This is achieved specifically by preparing people for particular occupations and generally by lowering the 'consciousness' of working people so that they come to accept the inevitability of their position as instruments for the achievement of ends over which they have no control or influence.

> In contrast, some generally more prosperous people follow a liberal-arts curriculum in a privately or neo-privately funded system. Such people compete to secure the prize of a high-status occupation which, at worst, ensures individual prosperity and for some, the opportunity to influence and form government policy. In Britain, an illusion of social mobility is maintained and promoted through schemes whereby a small number of poorer children are subsidised by others to attend private schools.[12]

> In America, it is claimed that the private housing market may be used to achieve mobility between generally poor, racially segregated state schools and more prosperous private schools that are generally located in suburban private housing schemes.[13] It is also worth noting that the spectacular success and media attention given to some business men[14] who proclaim their 'failure' at school, further maintains an illusion of social mobility. The net result is that there is effectively a two tier educational system — a state sector dominated by the idea of a vocational preparation for low-income itinerant occupations and a private sector[15] dominated by a liberal arts curriculum leading to high income permanent occupation and the benefits of curricular breadth and promotion of personal autonomy that are traditionally associated with such a curriculum.

The idea of a 'free market' as a fair and neutral arbiter in determining educational opportunity is in reality a myth. Instead the 'market' may be and is manipulated by government to suit its economic priorities. Therefore educational and economic policy are inextricably linked. Without some transformation of economic relations, it is impossible for educational policy successfully to address some of the problems of social inequality, injustice and lack of opportunity that are present within capitalist democracies.

Writers such as M.W. Apple, H.A. Giroux, S. Arnowitz, S. Bowles and H. Gintis might accept such a theory. These writers offer a far richer analysis of our present educational predicament than the one given above. Yet as Arnowitz and Giroux write:

> In our view, most exciting critical accounts of schooling fail to provide forms of analyses that move beyond theories of critique to the more difficult task of laying the theoretical basis for *transformative* modes of curriculum theory and practice.[16] (my emphasis)

These writers go on to advance the idea of teachers as 'transformative intellectuals'. In a similar vein, some writers advance the more-practical argument that teachers should become 'action researchers'.[17] One such writer complains:

> But while the body of Marxist and Neo-Marxist educational critique provides us with a radical alternative as far as the foundations of curriculum theory is concerned, it often leaves the 'structure' of the alternative curriculum to the imagination. That is, it is not always easy to answer the question 'What will I do on Monday?' from the curriculum theorizing of the 'new left'.[18]

While it is not clear that it can ever be easy to answer a question as context specific as this, it is becoming increasingly apparent (to theorists, if not to policy-makers) that theorizing about education is itself a practical activity that has practical implications for teaching. The idea that teachers should act simply as instrumental technicians for whom the only relevant theory concerns methodology, is now being replaced by the idea that teachers have something interesting to say about values and the aims of education.[19] This replacement coincides with the emergence of the idea of teachers as 'action researchers'.

This book is about the relationship between educational theory and practice and while the arguments advanced in it are critical of the notions of consumerism, managerialism and vocationalism, my analysis is primarily epistemological, that is, it is concerned primarily with assumptions about the nature of educational knowledge. I argue that the ideas of teachers as 'action researchers' and 'transformative intellectuals' or 'curriculum as praxis'[20] are bound to lack the context for their concrete realization as long as present institutional structures are rooted in a mistaken and alien epistemology. However, a new epistemology should be flexible enough to accommodate the idea of 'transformative' curriculum theory and practice. For me, this means that all arguments in favour of innovation must be located within the same epistemological framework that underpins the *status quo*.

This seems to lead to a paradox. On the one hand I argue that present institutional structures are rooted in a mistaken epistemology that prevents the concrete realization of curriculum theory that is meant to be transformative, yet on the other hand I argue that successful transformative theory must be located within that mistaken epistemology. The notion of 'hermeneutics' or 'interpretation' enables me to resolve this apparent paradox. I argue that theories are not compared in abstraction against some permanent criteria for truth or success. Rather, theories are compared by their proponents interpreting what each other is doing and continually reformulating criteria for theory comparison within a living shared context.

Therefore, my arguments are directed not only against what we might call 'market-managerialism' but also against those critics who write as if a mass theoretical conversion to a new epistemological framework could be achieved on the basis of theoretical discussion that floats free of the institutional contexts within which people work. However compelling these criticisms are, they lack the 'language of possibility',[21] to use a phrase of Arnowitz and Giroux. It is ironical that the idea of theoretical detachment underpins both educational policies that encapsulate market-managerialism and some criticism of these policies. While I criticize these policies, I do so from an epistemological perspective that views theory and practice as co-extensive. I believe that a common view of knowledge underpins both the position taken by proponents of market-managerialism and the position taken by those radical critics who seem to be waiting for a new evaluative framework to arrive as if theory could only go so far without some mass conversion to a set of values that embraces their critique.

I consider this polarization of views to be a subset of a more general philosophical dichotomy. I also consider that the polarization of views between market-managerialism and some accounts of liberalism to be sub-sets of this more general dichotomy. These sub-sets may be seen as two variants of a prior set of shared assumptions about the nature of knowledge. I argue that these assumptions are mistaken and attempt to articulate an alternative that leaves room for the idea that curricular choices are best viewed as choices about the superiority of rival theories rather than opposing dichotomies. For example, it seems to me to be unhelpful to see education as something detached from the worlds of business and commerce and free from concerns about 'market demand'. Equally though, I argue that it is unhelpful to see education as an endeavour that should be dominated by the supposed demands of industry, commerce or the 'market'.

I outline, instead, an epistemology that helps me to locate particular educational problems within a more general debate about theory-preference — a debate that is sustained in the work of W.V.O. Quine, T.S. Kuhn, R. Rorty, R.J. Bernstein, C. Taylor, A. MacIntyre and others. If my arguments are important, then it seems to me that they contribute to an updating of the epistemological underpinnings of educational theory so that educational practices might be seen to be informed by and debated with reference to theories that are evaluative as well as methodological. This opens up the possibility of resolving conflicts of value without getting stuck in a mire of either/or argument. Such a mire may lead theorists to try to secure the patronage of the powerful at the expense of the quality and breadth of their practice. On my view, educational policies may be compared and selected as if they were theories. Hence there is the possibility that educational policy might develop rationally on the basis of theoretical comparison. Recent events and revelations in Eastern Europe ought to worry those pragmatists who seem to take the *status quo* as inviolable and who decry theoretical reflection and justification as an expensive waste of time.

Overview of Argument

I begin by giving a brief background to the educational theory-practice debate in order to show that the problems with liberalism were inherent in the way in which it was interpreted by certain educational philosophers in the 60s, namely that it was interpreted in an empiricist way. I argue that this interpretation became entrenched within the institutional arrangements for theorizing about education and that this entrenchment has not been disturbed very much to date.

I go on to criticize empiricist epistemology on the grounds that 'experience' cannot provide the foundations necessary to support the claim that scientific knowledge is 'objective' knowledge. I argue that the dominance of this epistemology for the practice of theorizing about education, combined with the philosophical criticism that can be directed against it, gives rise either to the idea that theories may be compared according to some permanent neutral set of criteria (objectivism) or the idea that such criteria do not exist and therefore all theories are equally valid (relativism).

I develop the opposition between relativism and objectivism throughout this study. A number of alternative forms of objectivism are considered and rejected for the reason that even if permanent neutral criteria for all claims to knowledge could be specified, the process of relating any particular claim to knowledge with those criteria would itself introduce a contingency, the elimination of which would generate a logically regressive chain of criteria.[22] I also reject a number of forms of relativism including the form that suggests that educational theories may only be pragmatic responses to immediate practical problems and may not challenge the conceptual contexts within which particular problems are framed.

In common with other writers such as R.J. Bernstein and R. Rorty, I argue that this opposition between objectivism and relativism is unhelpful in our attempts to theorize about a world that is radically contingent. We argue that any attempt to ground our claims to knowledge either through empiricist notions such as the correspondence theory of truth[23] or through rationalist notions of permanent neutral sets of criteria for theory preference is bound to fail. Instead I follow Bernstein who suggests that we need

> a more historically situated, nonalgorithmic, flexible understanding of human rationality ... 'objectivism' as the basic conviction that there is or must be some permanent, ahistorical matrix or framework to which we can ultimately appeal in determining the nature of rationality ... is illusory.[24]

And Rorty who suggests that we are coming to the end of

the Kantian tradition that to be a philosopher is to have a 'theory of knowledge', and the Platonic tradition that action not based on knowledge of the truth of propositions is 'irrational' ... epistemology as the attempt to render all discourses commensurable by translating them into a preferred set of terms is unlikely to be a useful strategy.[25]

Recently, as Bernstein notes, there has been a 'convergence' of philosophical interest in the topics of objectivism and relativism. In this climate he suggests that 'hermeneutics' might offer a way out of the impasse suggested by the hold that objectivism and relativism have on our thinking. In the final part of this study I further the idea that 'hermeneutics' can offer us a way out of the impasse thrown up by notions of objectivism and relativism when theorizing about education.

I argue that trans-cultural judgments of rationality can be made in favour of 'scientific' societies rather than 'primitive' societies on the basis of the technological successes of the former that command the attention of the latter in a way that is not reciprocated. Within scientific societies, it is widely believed that natural scientific theories offer predictive and explanatory success that might well be achieved by other types of theorists if they were to emulate the procedures that natural scientists are assumed to follow. In the case of educational theorizing, however, there seems to have been an attempt to emulate a so called 'empirical' research procedure as if such a procedure were unquestionably responsible for the 'success' of the natural sciences.

In contrast to this notion, I hold that this research procedure is not responsible for the 'success' of the natural sciences. Instead, it is more plausible to attribute this 'success' to the way in which natural scientists incorporate their interpretations of what each of them is doing within a developing network of theory whose coherence is maximized according to the common values that bind the natural scientific community together. Moreover, a network of natural scientific theories cannot develop in isolation from networks of other types of theory because the explanatory power of scientific terms is parasitic upon what we might call a 'family resemblance' relation subsisting between scientific and non-scientific forms of discourse. There is, instead, a 'linguistic division of labour'[26] both within the natural scientific community and across to other communities of theorists. Hence I believe that educational theorists should emulate this 'hermeneutic' account of natural scientific research.

Since the notion of interpretation takes on a central importance for my account of educational theory, I discuss this notion in connection with H.G. Gadamer's notion of 'hermeneutics' and J. Habermas's extension of that notion. Both writers stress that theory has its moment of application in practice, that is to say that both writers stress that it is in the process of interpreting another theory that one's own practical orientation shifts. Yet they differ in their suggestions as to how far it is both possible and desirable to go towards objectivism in the choice of rival interpretations. I take a position somewhere between Gadamer's suggestion that ultimately we just act or decide in the same way as we might decide that we like a particular painting or decide what to do, on the spur of the moment, as it were, and Habermas's suggestion that, when we come to a decision, we are motivated by a concern that that decision would command a 'consensus' in the 'ideal' situation in which all interested persons are free to contribute to a discussion without the existence of any form of domination or coercion.

I adapt Habermas's notion of an 'ideal consensus' in order to explain how theorizing can be something other than a pragmatic response to immediate problems. I argue that the 'ideal consensus' is a 'regulative ideal' that guides every attempt to theorize and so every theorist is able to place in jeopardy not just those claims that are assumed by the framework within which the theorist is working but also the framework itself. Unless the theorist recognizes this difficulty, then achieving an 'ideal consensus' may simply reinforce the values and norms that underpin the framework. For example, a feminist might argue that even if a community of people, dedicated to the notion of an 'ideal consensus' were formed, our language is so loaded with male dominated terms, that the consensus itself, however sympathetic to feminist ideals, necessarily reinforces male values and norms. For that and other reasons I do not accept Habermas's idea that the 'ideal consensus' is a notion that can be made theoretically explicit in order to function as a foundation for all forms of interpretation; for this idea seems to me to be another form of objectivism that leads our educational thinking back to a concern to find that set of educational theories that form a set of exclusive guides to rational practice.

My educational thesis may be seen to parallel Rorty's[27] philosophical thesis that traditional concerns with the nature of certainty stem from an unwarranted search for security in a contingent universe. Just as Rorty advocates a less ambitious but more valuable role for philosophy as a tool for cultural criticism in the service of the 'ungrounded social hope' that human life can be improved, so too I attempt to avoid what, on my argument, is a waste of effort in trying to mould educational practices according to the latest version of objectivism as it might be applied to educational practices, whether that version purports to be provided by criterion referenced assessment, performance criteria for curricular evaluation or the special training of managers who might be supposed to ensure the achievement of objectives set by those who have a distant concern with the practice of teaching. Instead, I argue that we do better to approach the conditions under which an 'ideal consensus' might be realized, sometimes by making those imaginative leaps that enable us to see the options that face us afresh and to act upon them with a confidence that is derived more from a feeling that we are acting 'in solidarity' with one another than from an impractical attempt to apply what purports to be the latest version of objectivism.

I conclude by outlining a transformative theory that attempts to show how the objectivism of market-managerialism might be challenged. Such challenge will always be risky in the sense that no one knows its precise nature or direction. However, I argue that unless we take risks, educational practice may remain ossified within a particular framework of enquiry and theory may be seen merely as a response to particular problems. It seems to me that the search for coherence that governs the development of a network of theory should include the possibility that within all endeavours, 'revolutionary' conceptual shifts may take place from time to time in a manner that is similar to the one that is supposed by Kuhn to take place in the case of natural science. To this end, I suggest that it may be helpful to distinguish between a (theoretical) search for coherence across a wide range of endeavours and a more limited (practical) search. That is not to elevate one type of search above the other. Rather it is to suggest that those who happen to occupy the role of theorist are seen as conversational partners with whom those who occupy the role of practitioners find it helpful to talk in order to make progress in their own search for holistic coherence. Even though this suggestion appears to be modest, I argue that a hermeneutic conception of educational theory has radical implications — for the teacher education curriculum, for curriculum generally and for managerial practices based on the notion of an educational 'market'.

Notes and References

1 National Commission on Excellence in Education (1985) 'A Nation at Risk' ch. 1 in GROSS, B. and GROSS, R. (Eds) *The Great School Debate.*
2 CALLAGHAN, J. Speech at Ruskin College, Oxford, 18 October 1976.
3 For an account of this concern and its effect in Britain see AINLEY, P. (1988) *From School to YTS*, especially chs. 5 and 6. cf. APPLE, M.W. (1986) *Teachers and Texts*, chs. 5 and 6.
4 Reported by AINLEY, P. 1988, p. 82.
5 Lord Young has often argued this point and it is embedded within many recent British Government publications, cf. HMSO (1985) *Better Schools* (Cmnd. 9469) and HMSO (1986) *Working Together — Education and Training* (Cmnd. 9823).
6 The Commissioners referred to in note 1 above were concerned with the decreasing inability of American industry to compete in the international market place. See also LEVIN, H.M. (1985) 'Education and jobs: The weak link', ch. 27 in GROSS, B. and GROSS, R. (Eds) *The Great School Debate.*
7 See AINLEY, P., 1988, p. 116 for an analysis of this demand in Britain. cf. KATZNELSON, I. and WEIR, M. (1985) *Schooling for All*, ch. 8 for an American analysis.
8 This is one of the arguments put forward by supporters of the idea of 'students loans'. These people argue that students should be prepared to invest in their own future prosperity.
9 The minority who manipulate the market essentially control the instrumental activities of the majority.
10 cf. BOWLES, S. and GINTIS, H. (1976) *Schooling in Capitalist America.*
11 CARR, W. (1989) 'The Idea of an Educational Science', p. 36.
12 I refer to the 'assisted places scheme'.
13 See KATZNELSON, I. and WEIR, M., 1985, ch. 8.
14 I am thinking here of people like Richard Branson, chairman of the Virgin group of companies and Alan Sugar, chairman of Amstrad.
15 Notice that the so-called 'opting out' legislation in Britain may be designed to privatize those schools that are predominantly middle-class and located in more prosperous areas.
16 ARNOWITZ, S. and GIROUX, H.A. (1986) *Education under Siege*, p. 154.
17 I evaluate the 'action research' movement in Chapter 5.
18 GRUNDY, S. (1987) *Curriculum: Product or Praxis*, p. 1.
19 WRINGE, C. (1988) *Understanding Educational Aims*, ch. 1 argues that the present tendency to account for educational shortcomings by referring to a teacher's lack of particular methodological skills is misleading. Instead he argues that these shortcomings may be attributed to a general sense of unease about the point of teaching particular lessons. He suggests that this uneasiness among teachers may extend as far as the general aims of present educational provision.
20 GRUNDY, S., 1987.
21 ARNOWITZ, S. and GIROUX, H.A., 1986, p. 154.
22 Readers who are not familiar with these ideas may find it helpful to consider the following example: when marking an examination script it

is usual to employ a marking scheme that is supposed to set out criteria for 'objectivity' in grading. Both the script and the scheme are interpreted and where these interpretations coincide the script is marked correct or incorrect. However in some circumstances, the interpretation may be problematic and markers look for further guidance. In effect they are looking for a further set of criteria that govern the interpretation of the marking scheme or first set of criteria, as it might be called. It is not difficult to see that this second set of criteria may require a third set of criteria for its interpretation and so on into what is called 'an infinite regress'. In practice, of course, the 'infinite regress' is avoided by an appeal to an authority such as a chief examiner. However this appeal weakens the case that the grading is 'objective'.

23   This is the theory that a proposition is true if it corresponds to the way things actually are in a world that is assumed to constitute an 'objective' reality.

24   BERNSTEIN, R.J. (1985) *Beyond Objectivism and Relativism*, p. xi.

25   RORTY, R. (1980) *Philosophy and the Mirror of Nature*, p. 356.

26   This is the title of a thesis put forward by PUTNAM, H. (1975) in 'The Meaning of Meaning', in his *Mind Language and Reality*, pp. 215–71.

27   See RORTY, R., 1980, and his *Consequences of Pragmatism*, 1982.

Chapter 1

Theoretical Origins

This chapter begins with a debate about educational theory that dominated philosophy of education during the 1960s and that continued well into the 1980s. This debate is important for three main reasons: first, it may serve as an introduction to some of the key philosophical issues that arise out of a consideration of the relationship between theory and practice. Second, I argue that this debate has left a legacy in the form of the normal institutional arrangements for training teachers and theorizing about education. Third, I argue that this debate is underpinned by an epistemology that also underpins many currently popular educational policies, theories and practices. As I shall argue in later chapters, this epistemology is radically mistaken, hence many currently popular educational practices should be changed so that they cohere with an alternative that I shall outline.

Perhaps the most well-known contributors to the previously-mentioned debate were P.H. Hirst and D.J. O'Connor.[1] These writers appear to disagree about the nature of educational theory. O'Connor argues that educational theory should be 'objective' and 'scientific' whereas Hirst seems to argue for a more pluralistic and evaluative conception of educational theory. However, Hirst is also one of the principal architects of a philosophy of education that is supposed to offer analytic truths about education. So while Hirst and O'Connor may disagree about the nature of educational theory, they may be seen to be united in an attempt to formulate true theories that should guide educational practice. Their disagreement may in fact be underpined by a common epistemology that separates facts from values and theory from practice. Since debate about educational theory in the 1960s was almost exclusively carried on within the framework set by this epistemology, it is not surprising that many people believed that institutions like the colleges and departments of education should produce theories that guide those who work within practical institutions like schools.

As Hirst's philosophy of education came under increasing attack, something like O'Connor's account of educational theory became more acceptable. Educational theorizing became dominated by concerns about methodology and empirical investigations by psycho-logists and sociologists became commonplace in the colleges and departments of education. The aims of the education system were entrenched within policies that were set by a minority not directly concerned with the practice of teaching and teachers were left with a role similar to that of a technician — the role of carrying out instruc-tions in the most efficient manner.

The Hirst-O'Connor Debate

O'Connor sought to promote the view that only empirical research can provide educational theory and further that such research is best modelled on the natural sciences which he believed supply us with 'objective' knowledge uncontaminated by personal beliefs and prejudices.[2] The assumption behind this view seems to be that there is a world external to us which we seek to describe with ever increasing accuracy; the better we describe this world then the better we can move around within it. However, as numerous attempts to articulate and justify correspondence theories of truth have shown, we do not have direct access to the way the world may be actually constructed and divided up. Indeed, we cannot make sense of the idea that the world is actually divided up in any way since whatever observation language we use presupposes its own way of dividing up the world. Furthermore, the success of predictions in the natural sciences is bound up with the fact that all states of the system under investigation can be described by the same concepts in the future as in the past, usually values of the same variables. However, in the social sciences the very terms in which the future will have to be characterized are not available at present and so it is perhaps not surprising that the sort of educational theory that O'Connor prescribed is not yet available.

Even if educational theory did supply empirical generalizations that enabled us to know *how* to do things, according to O'Connor educational theory would still not enable us to know what we *ought* to do.[3] Theory would give us a guide to *means* but not *ends*. O'Con-nor considered that the selection of ends involves making value judg-ments for which there is no support emanating from his account of educational theory. The import of values into educational theory he considered to be 'both unnecessary and logically disastrous'.[4] It is logically disastrous because for O'Connor there is no logical relationship between values let alone between values and empirical theory; and it is unnecessary because if we do incorporate values into educational theory then we gain no advantage since our theory still only 'guides' our practice and we incur the penalty that our theory becomes an 'intellectual salad'[5] which incurs 'the logical odium of begging disputed questions that are central to moral philosophy'.[6]

There are three points that arise from this version of theory by O'Connor that are worth noting. First, there is his supposition that moral philosophy is completely devoid of logical reasoning — that either an argument conforms to the canons of deductive logic or else it is not logical at all. This seems highly contentious in that it seems to deny that there might be any point in doing moral philosophy. Moreover, it is logically disastrous for O'Connor to be advancing a meta-theoretical analysis designed to warn us not to take the vaporizing of evaluative theorists seriously, when such an analysis is itself an attempt to promote the value of a particular type of reasoning.

The mistake that I think that O'Connor makes is to assume that there is only one form of reasoning, empirical reasoning, that sets the criteria by which all other forms of reasoning can be judged. Since moral 'reasoning' so-called does not meet these criteria, O'Connor considers it to be outside logic. However, as Mill wrote in connection with the idea that there might be moral proof:

> It is evident that there cannot be proof in the ordinary or popular meaning of the term. Questions of ultimate ends are not amenable to direct proof ... We are not, however, to infer that its acceptance or rejection must depend on blind impulse, or arbitrary choice.[7]

O'Connor must presumably agree with this for, in putting forward a view of what educational theory should do, O'Connor is acquiescing in the idea that there is at least one way in which an argument for some desirable end can be formulated.

The second point to note is the idea that theory should guide practice in some way. O'Connor seemed to mean that just as physical theory provides 'a guidance system for the applied physicist and engineer'[8] so psychological and sociological theory might be supposed to provide a guidance system for the teacher. However, while there is undoubtedly some relationship between physical theory and engineering artefacts, the logic of that relationship is not at all clear since the least applied research can often lead to a proliferation of unexpected artefacts, as in the case of Einstein's special theory of relativity.[9] It depends, therefore, what O'Connor meant by 'a guidance system'. The weak sense of 'guidance' illustrated by the physics-engineering example is unhelpful to practitioners since it is the expected outcomes that are of interest to them. The alternative is to adopt a strong sense of 'guidance' that supposes that theory will consist of a series of conditional statements of the form 'if such and such a state is desired then perform such and such a series of tasks'. The problem with this sense of guidance is that it presupposes that both states and tasks can be precisely specified in advance of the situation to which they will apply. There is also the practical difficulty of knowing just how much detail and how many conditionals are required.

O'Connor seemed to accept that neither sense of guidance is satisfactory when he admitted that

> even if theories of education did meet these exacting standards (of scientific theory), it is doubtful if they would yield the same kind of practical advances that technology, medicine and economic organisations owe to their respective bases.[10]

He suggested that this is partly because

> effective education is quite possible without any of the theoretical background of the kind offered by psychology, sociology and the rest of the relevant sciences. And this is not the case with medicine and engineering.[11]

This statement reveals the way that O'Connor seemed to regard educational practice as something that exists independently of any educational theory, whereas he seemed to suppose that theories of medicine and engineering serve to differentiate medical or engineering practice from some other and unrelated things like witchdoctoring or basic craft. O'Connor misses the point that we need some means of identifying when educational practice is taking place and neglects the account of theory that suggests that to have a theory is to have an idea of what does and what does not count as a practice.

The third point to be noted is the assumed separation of means from ends with the claim that while decisions about ends are outside of logic, and hence for O'Connor rationality, means can be determined rationally on the basis of weighing up the scientific facts. This notion of means-ends rationality can be seen to be at work in much of what presently goes on in educational institutions by way of curriculum planning. First, the desirable ends or objectives are determined. Presently this is often done by 'analyzing needs'. That is to say that the satisfaction of the perceived needs of some client group become the objectives of the enterprise. The objectives are then made 'operational' which means either that they are 'reduced' to statements of behaviour or that they are 'reduced' so that they are amenable to testing by questionnaire or structured interview. Second, the methods and procedures are determined on the basis of the empirical evidence available. Finally, the effectiveness of the teaching or course or whatever is determined by the extent to which the objectives have been met and in the light of any discrepancies new methods and procedures are tried out.

This notion of means-ends curriculum planning has been discussed in most books on 'curriculum development'[12] and is discussed more fully in my next chapter. For the moment, it is worth noting that means-ends curriculum planning suffers from serious drawbacks, such as the adequacy of reductions of mental states to behavioural statements,[13] the adequacy of experimental techniques such as questionnaires to measure complex educational objectives and the difficulty if not impossibility of detailing predicted future outcomes with conceptual tools subject to revision.[14] It is considerations like these that prompt Barrow,[15] for example, to suggest that time would be better spent thinking through the implications of a proposal prior to its implementation rather than going through this procedure of post evaluation. There is finally the difficulty that Rizvi[16] describes with the idea that evaluative discourse can be settled once and for all and combined with factual judgments, as if factual judgments were not made on the basis of normative criteria or evaluative discourse was not influenced by causal explanatory relations.

Let us turn now to Hirst's account of educational theory by recalling his 'forms of knowledge' thesis and the role that philosophy takes within it. Hirst argues that knowledge consists of a limited number of quite distinct forms that can be distinguished logically on the basis of three criteria;

1 The central concepts that are peculiar to the forms.
2 The distinctive logical structure or relationship among concepts.
3 the criteria for truth or validity.[17]

Hirst's account of the scientific form seems to agree roughly with O'Connor's account of science. However Hirst argues that not only science but also any combination of the forms can provide an educational theory which provides 'rational principles for educational practice'.[18] Thus educational theory is concerned with both the formulation of ultimate educational ends as well as the discovery of efficient means.

However, it is not clear how forms that are supposed to be distinct can combine to form the practical theory that Hirst seeks. Hirst cannot have it both ways. Either the forms are logically distinct (which Hirst needs them to be in order to justify his idea of a liberal education) but at the price of rendering his account of educational theory implausible; or else the forms of knowledge can be synthesized, in which case the argument for logical separation disappears and we are still left with an unsatisfactory account of educational theory. In either case we still have the empirical difficulty of finding an individual or group with a broad command of knowledge in all its forms to draw up the rational principles for practice that Hirst requires.

As for O'Connor, the idea of 'rational principles for practice' is problematic for it is not clear what form these are to take or indeed if there are such principles. In *The Concept of Mind*[19] Ryle attacks the notion that decisions about what to do necessarily precede action — as if rationality is always secured when a series of deliberations about the application of universal principles precedes a series of actions. It is not hard to find many examples of people's doing things, of which it makes little sense to say that their practice is somehow guided by theories that are rehearsed in the mind: for instance, riding a bicycle, playing the part of a clown, or even teaching! Even if such theories could be formulated there would still be the problem of distinguishing between good and bad theory. In other words, there would still be a need to provide criteria for theory preference. Arguably there are plenty of educational theories about but unless we have some idea of how educational theories are evaluated and even how to describe theories in logically compatible terms then we have no guide to practice whatever. Moreover, further theories would seem to be needed to guide the application of the original set of theories with the need for further theories to apply the second set of theories and so on.

In a recent publication Hirst admits to some of these difficulties. While being 'unrepentant in seeing educational theory as primarily the domain which seeks to develop rational principles for educational practice',[20] he now seems to recognize the importance of practice and the significance of the tacit elements in all action.[21] Despite this admission and the numerous objections that have been directed against his forms of knowledge thesis,[22] Hirst's account of educational theory was more widely accepted than that of O'Connor. Part of this acceptance was no doubt due to the prominence of the account of philosophical knowledge that Hirst, along with Peters, articulated, that is meant to cohere with and to some extent underpin both the forms of knowledge thesis and Hirst's account of educational theory. According to Hirst and Peters, philosophy is a form of knowledge that is concerned to find the 'logically necessary conditions for the use of a word'.[23] These conditions are to be identified via the process of linguistic analysis. This process results in what has been called Analytic Philosophy of Education (APE). According to some recent accounts, APE has been so influential that any research in philosophy of education that did not conform to APE's rhetorical norms and interests could be excluded.[24]

Analytic Philosophy of Education

APE is alleged to arise out of Wittgenstein's later philosophy which paradoxically can be seen as an attack on the idea of a theory.

> If I were told that anything were a theory, I would say, No, No! That does not interest me — it would not be the exact thing I was looking for. . . .
>   For me the theory has no value. A theory gives me nothing.[25]

This apparent anti-theoretic view can be traced back to Wittgenstein's challenge to us to find the essence of something. For example, in the *Philosophical Investigations*[26] his imaginary interlocutor accuses him of nowhere saying what the essence of a language game is. Wittgenstein replies

> and this is true — instead of producing something common to all that we call language, I am saying that these phenomena have no one thing in common which makes us use the same word for all, but that they are related to one another in many different ways.

In *Philosophical Investigations* *19–23* Wittgenstein invites us to find what is common to the proceedings that we call games and suggests that there is no one thing that is 'common to all, but similarities, relationships, and a whole series of them at that'. Later he characterizes these similarities as 'family resemblances'.

This seems straightforward yet it seems to rule out as a valid method of philosophy that version of it that attempts to discover those properties which all members of a class may be deemed to possess. The denial of the validity of this form of what has been called essentialism goes against that tradition of philosophical theorizing which produces grand theories that attempt to simplify and maximize coherence. Instead, Wittgenstein suggests that many so-called philosophical problems simply disappear if the words that are used to pose the problem are returned to their natural base.

> When philosophers use a word — 'knowledge', 'being', 'object', 'I', 'proposition', 'name', — and try to grasp the *essence* of the thing, one must always ask oneself: is the word ever actually used in the language game which is its original home? — What *we* do is to bring words back from their metaphysical to their everyday use.[27] (original emphasis)

This has been taken by some to mean that philosophers should act as a kind of 'thought police'[28] who prevent people from wandering off the road of common sense which has special epistemic privilege. The function of such 'thought police' is to analyze linguistic practice in order to find the 'logically necessary conditions for the use of a word'.[29] Thus Wittgenstein's later philosophy may be seen to suggest a philosophical method which proceeds by way of analysis of the various ways that words are used in order to elucidate the 'correct' or 'standard' use. This is the method assumed by APEs. However, it is not at all clear that Wittgenstein intended to suggest a method of analysis that guaranteed the correct use of words. Rather, there is some reason to suppose that Wittgenstein neither intended to suggest a philosophical method nor even any philosophical theses.

The distinction between 'saying' and 'showing' which was made initially in the *Tractatus*[30] has been traced through to *On Certainty*.[31] In the *Tractatus*, philosophical propositions, were regarded as being amongst those that could only be shown not said. However, since the *Tractatus* consists of philosophical propositions then it seems as if Wittgenstein is stating that which, by his own propositions, could only be shown. The metaphor of a ladder has been taken to be a device whereby Wittgenstein accounts for his own thesis.

> My propositions serve as elucidations in the following way: anyone who understands me eventually recognizes them as nonsensical, when he has used them — as steps — to climb up beyond them. (He must, so to speak, throw away the ladder after he has climbed up it.)[32]

It seems that the *Tractatus* cannot on this logic consist of philosophical propositions. Rather it consists of metaphorical allusions to a philo-sophical thesis. In Wittgenstein's later philosophy, there is a similar insistence on the alleged unstatability of philosophy. The style of presentation is unusual and it is argued that this style was chosen in order not to appear to suggest a statement of philosophical theses. Rather it has been argued that the style was carefully chosen to have the most chance of changing the reader's way of seeing the world.[33]

If this is true then perhaps it is the lack of a suitable context for philosophical remarks that prompted Wittgenstein's pessimistic com-ments about being misunderstood.

> I was obliged to learn that my results (which I had communi-cated in lectures, typescripts and discussions), variously mis-understood, more or less mangled or watered down, were in circulation.[34]

Furthermore it is possible to argue that Wittgenstein's later enigmatic and aphoristic style was designed to 'lock out' those who could not understand. This idea may be supported by reference to passages of *Culture and Value* where Wittgenstein[35] writes of forms of presentation including that of the image of a lock to which only those with a key can get inside. Wittgenstein goes on to complain that Freud's theories are so easily unlocked that everybody has access to 'fanciful pseudo explanations'.[36]

It looks as if there are good reasons for believing that the style of Wittgenstein's writing is designed to exclude those unable to under-stand it. Now if the difficulty in understanding is derived from the impossibility of stating the showable, then it looks as if only those 'on the inside', so to speak, will understand. By stressing the tacitness of philosophy, Wittgensteinians seem to be suggesting that criticism implies lack of understanding; understanding implies allegiance.[37]

Many find this form of 'insider-dealing' unacceptable.[38] These critics seem united in their belief that rationality depends upon the clear statement of theses which are understandable and open to refutation by anyone. For these critics 'tacitness' is a threat to rationality, hence they attempt to objectify the 'tacit' by describing it in as precise a way as possible.[39] However, as I shall argue in Chapter 4, this form of objectivism is impossible. Instead, I argue that we should do better to acknowledge that some human experiences including some educational experiences cannot be usefully described.

APEs may be seen to have made two kinds of mistake. First, if Wittgenstein wrote in an enigmatic way in order to proffer a carefully chosen 'key' to his thoughts, then there seems to be some impropriety in trying to reveal the postulated Wittgensteinian method and apply it to an area like education. Second, even when APEs have attempted to find and state analytic theses by analysis of ordinary talk about education, their role is the doubtful 'second order' one of clarifying talk about education in preparation for or as a subsidiary to 'first-order' attempts to say something substantive.[40]

The nature of this so-called 'second order' activity has been characterized as stemming from the 'underlabourer' conception. This conception was introduced by Locke in his *Essay Concerning Human Understanding*[41] in order to draw an analogy between the work of 'master builders' and great scientists like Newton, Huyghens and Boyle. Locke argued that, just as the progress of master builders is enhanced when the ground is cleared for them by underlabourers, so scientific progress would be enhanced if 'underlabourers' in the form of 'philosophers' were to clear away

> some of the rubbish that lies in the way to knowledge [like] the learned but frivolous use of uncouth, affected, or unintelligible terms.[42]

Within APE philosophy is widely viewed as a sort of ground clearing operation that takes place separately from any substantive theorizing about education. But as Aspin remarks, this view has tended to lead to

> a dismissive attitude to the deliberations of philosophers who, it was felt, were contributing little if anything to the solution of the problems with which teachers in schools had daily to contend.[43]

The problem for APE is that, in producing analytic truths by analysis of everyday use of language, it has to select what is going to count as everyday use. In order to identify the everyday use of educational words APE needs some idea of what 'education' is. The question arises as to whether APE's idea of education is the same as anybody else's idea, and if it is not, then there is the problem of selecting the 'correct use'. Putting it more strongly it does not seem possible for APE to avoid the charge that its method simply reinforces its prior commitment to certain values and norms. Furthermore, it has been argued that analysis does not take place in a vacuum with universal criteria of correctness. Instead analysis takes place at particular times, for particular purposes; and again as Aspin remarks

> the prime problem of analysis is . . . the elucidation of the very theoretical foundations upon which a particular analysis or view of analysis rests.[44]

As a result of these and other criticisms, APE may be seen to have retreated into the role of modest supporter of the task of producing a conceptualization of a research problem prior to empirical research taking place. While Hirst and O'Connor's views of educational theory seem opposed, they can in fact be seen to reinforce each other within a common epistemology — that of foundational empiricism. Within this epistemology both Hirst and O'Connor seem to suggest that value-free knowledge about education is possible. In the case of O'Connor, educational 'facts' are supposedly ascertained by following the methods claimed by positivists to be those characteristic of natural science. In the case of Hirst, analysis of educational language is supposed to guarantee the 'correct' or 'standard' application of words, supposedly by following the later philosophy of Wittgenstein.

Both views of educational theory offer the possibility of enhanced status to the purveyors of 'facts' or analytic 'correctness', for if rational action depends upon knowledge of the 'facts' or analytic 'correctness' then educational theorists seem to be the putative guardians of educational rationality. I suggest that the legacy of Hirst and O'Connor is so entrenched in *much* current educational theorizing that it sets the parameters within which much research, curriculum design and evaluation take place. In particular we seem to be left with the isolation of educational policy from both theory and practice which is reflected in the institutional arrangements within which each is carried out. Let us now examine the nature of the epistemology that underpins these arrangements.

Empiricist Foundationalist Epistemology

The idea that knowledge could be based on secure foundations can in modern times be traced back at least as far as Descartes' search for some indubitable premise secure enough to hold the weight of all other premises that can be logically deduced from it.[45] Much of our present idea of the relationship between knowledge, certainty and doubt can be traced back to this 'foundationalist' idea.

While we may *believe* that something is the case, many philosophers — for example Woozley, Ayer, Scheffler — hold that we can only be said to *know* it if we can justify our belief against rational doubt by giving a series of reasons that can be traced back to something (a foundation or a stop) which is held to be certain. If we cannot do this we end up with an infinite regress of reasons and are in the disastrous position of having to know an infinite number of things before anything can be known. The regress is usually halted in one of two ways. Empiricists see the regress halting at the level of sense data whereas rationalists see the regress halting at their postulate of some sort of innate knowledge. The problem for empiricists is that our senses sometimes deceive us. Descartes' solution to this problem was to posit a benevolent God who would ensure that our senses were not invariably deceived.[46]

A more recent solution is to deny the validity of foundationalism and with it to deny the coherence of universal doubt by arguing that doubt only makes sense against a background of certainty. In other words, if most things were not certain then it would not be possible to have a concept of doubt. Since ordinary language seems to presuppose that most things are certain then an acceptance of the epistemic authority of ordinary language seems to suggest that universal doubt is incoherent. However, this argument relies upon our acceptance that ordinary language has epistemic authority, and while this may be true for medium-sized physical objects as Wittgenstein argues in *On Certainty*,[47] it is not necessarily universally true unless with Wittgenstein we accept that science forms the basis of a 'system of belief' and agree in turn that the existence of medium-sized physical objects forms the basis of our science. The difficulty with Wittgenstein's argument is that it seems to lead to relativism in that truth seems to be relative to a 'system of belief'.

The phenomenalist answer to the problem of finding a foundation for knowledge (as in empiricism) suffers from the difficulty that a sense datum is neither true nor false and so cannot function as a foundation. Sense data need to be recorded as propositions but the gap between proposition and datum is sufficient to allow doubt to creep back in. We seem either to have to accept that individual introspection is always reliable though, as well as being implausible, this position is also incomprehensible if we follow Wittgenstein's discussion regarding sensations — his 'Sensation S'.[48] Alternatively, we have to appeal to science to justify our perceptual experience but this involves us in appealing to science to justify science and this circularity gets us no further with making sense of foundational empiricism.

It is worth noting the irony in APEs accepting the conceptual-empirical distinction which is embedded within foundationalist empiricism while APE itself is supposedly derived from Wittgenstein's later philosophy, one of whose main thrusts is to deny the very distinction which APEs accept. Nevertheless the idea of man alone in the world picking up sense data, organizing the data to produce knowledge of the world and making decisions about what to do in the world on the basis of that knowledge is a very powerful idea. On the other hand, as Holland has argued, empiricism tends to lead to 'stunted epistemology and no philosophy of education worth mentioning'.[49] This is because the empiricist need only be exposed to the world, not to other people with whom the individual might interact, in order to understand. In other words, empiricism seems to leave language as something that will take care of itself.

Perhaps another reason apart from the perceived absence of an alternative, for the continued acceptance of foundational empiricism by some educational theorists, is the recent interest shown in cybernetic models of learning and 'information technology'. The possibility afforded by technological advance that much more information could be made more easily accessible to more people has tended to reinforce empiricist accounts of rationality. This is because the empiricist idea that rational decision-making depends upon taking into account all the relevant 'facts' was always damaged by the empirical impossibility of actually getting hold of all of the facts. The advent of the 'information technology revolution' seems to have turned this impossibility into a mere technical difficulty. In addition, recent developments in Artificial Intelligence have suggested to some psychologists[50] that the system whereby a computer inputs information, processes it according to a program and outputs a signal which is translated by robotics into action, could provide a useful and informative contrast to the way a human being might input information using the senses, process it according to 'cognitive structure' and output signals neurophysiologically to muscles in order to act.

On this view educational theory may well be concerned with

refining the models of learning we operate with, as is for example the case with Papert's[51] concern with the elimination of 'bugs' in thinking. Papert suggests that the computer programmer's concept of 'bug' is a 'powerful idea' that enables us to think more confidently and effectively. Alternatively, educational theory can be regarded as concerned with the elaboration of the material conditions assumed by the model. Interestingly it is the construction and production of hardware and software necessary for efficient speech recognition and translation systems that seem to be the most difficult set of material conditions to elaborate.[52] Perhaps this difficulty is parallelled by the problem that the ideas that human meaning poses for social scientists and perhaps this is why some educational theorists have accepted the shortcut that APE seems to offer.

I suggest that educational research may be likened to empiricist versions of physical scientific research if APEs take on the task of hypostatizing meaning. Just as physical scientific research is supposed to proceed by isolating variables, varying experimental conditions, making causal connections and drawing conclusions between variables that can be acted upon, so too educational research may be supposed to proceed in the same way. However, educational researchers are faced with special difficulties when attempting to isolate the variables: first, there is the difficulty of accounting for extraneous variables, but perhaps the most serious difficulty concerns the application of the research. Since the very terms in which the future will have to be characterized are not yet necessarily all available to the researcher at the time at which he completes his research, the research findings may have little practical relevance. I suggest that APE, seen as the activity of 'ground clearing' that takes place prior to and separate from the actual empirical research, has been widely regarded as capable of fulfilling the equivalent of the 'isolation of variables' stage of the empiricist research procedure. By offering the possibility of hypostatizing meaning, APE has been supposed to guarantee that the assignation of the variables could be held constant throughout the research and its application so that the researchers could proceed according to models apotheosized by a commitment to empiricist epistemology and procedure.

APE can thus be seen to purport to offer the theoretical foundations for what is often referred to as 'the conceptualization of a research problem'. There remains the idea that analysis of language can enable the educational researcher to overcome the sort of problems that seem to trouble some other social scientists such as the importance of taking into account intention and purpose. The articulation of the APE research programme can thus be seen to support and reinforce empiricist epistemology.

Furthermore, just as physical scientific research is supposed to provide knowledge or theory which guides practice (for example, isolate the variables pressure and depth, measure pressure and depth under various conditions, discover a relationship, conclude that pressure increases linearly with depth: therefore when diving wear a pressure suit), so too educational theory is supposed to guide practice. However, the auxiliary hypotheses, the procedures of manufacture, the agreed methods of testing that characterize the diving suit example, seem to be missing in the educational case and so even if the empiricist research procedure were itself adequate there would still be no practical guidance of the type sought. The frequent requests for greater relevance of educational research and theory[53] and frequent complaints about the value of studying much of what counts as theory in some colleges and departments of education[54] might be related to these deficiencies in empiricist epistemology and research procedures.

I am arguing that while APE is supposedly derived from Wittgenstein's later philosophy, much of which is directed against foundational empiricism, APE can in fact be viewed as a sort of lifebuoy which has kept empiricist educational research afloat. This can be illustrated by reference to J. Wilson's *Philosophy and Educational Research*.[55] Wilson argues that educational research in 1972 was in a mess and that 'a good deal of the work of research in Education will have to be done from scratch'.[56] Despite this prescription and the passing of fourteen or so years, there is reason to suppose that Wilson would argue and prescribe in the same way today. Indeed, much of his output is still concerned to correct what he sees is the lamentable state of educational theory and research.[57] While Wilson accepts the importance of empirical research, he argues that researchers spend too little time thinking about what the parameters of their research might mean and too little time listening to what philosophers were telling them about the importance of 'conceptual clarity'. Apparently, empirical research is all right as long as it is remembered that it involves conceptual matters which are philosophical concerns. Implicit in Wilson's work is the commitment to the still accepted tenet of the necessary conceptual-empirical distinction and with it the necessity of a shared responsibility in educational research between psychologists, sociologists and philosophers. The 'underlabourer' conception of philosophy is again apparent here and it is not hard to see that in times of economic stringency, researchers of an empirical persuasion might train themselves to do their own conceptual clarification. It might be felt that the employment of professionally-trained philosophers was something of an indulgence in such 'hard times'.

The Professionalization of Educational Theory

We have seen how a disagreement over the nature of educational theory is underpinned by common assumptions about the nature of knowledge and how this disagreement might have served to reinforce the view that professionally privileged theorists should do research and produce theories that are designed to guide the practice of teachers. As a result, all prospective educational practitioners would seem to need to pass through the theorist's tutelage as an initiation[58] into teaching. This initiation might enable trainees to learn educational theories prior to their application. The idea that an 'immersion' in psychological, sociological and philosophical theory with perhaps a touch of history might help to prepare practitioners was institutionalized in the colleges and departments of education of the 1960s and early 1970s.

We have seen, too, that as APE started to decline (perhaps because people became bored with endless analyses of terms like education, indoctrination and autonomy,[59] perhaps also because people came to question the relevance of these analyses and to expose some of the inconsistencies within APE), APE may be seen to have retreated from its more substantive theses of liberalism and rationalism to the more modest role of 'underlabourer' to empirical research. There is more than a small change in the division of labour at stake here. The weakening of APE led to the resurrection of something like O'Connor's version of the nature of educational theory with the 'analysis of language' thesis supporting it. 'Educational theory' became knowledge about the most efficient method of carrying out some predetermined and self-referential policy. The institutional arrangements that were partly legitimated by the theorist's claim to supply 'transcendental' arguments, 'logical' requirements and 'correct' analyses were now helpful in reinforcing the claim of empirical researchers to supply 'objective' knowledge about educational methods that might provide temporary foundations upon which to rest justificatory claims about educational practice.

As a result, theory may now be seen to be in the middle of a three-way split of policy, theory and practice with policy-makers assuming exclusive responsibility for the formulation of educational aims and with theorists attempting to work out the most efficient means of achieving those aims. The institutional arrangements that previously were set up to reflect the theorist's position as the supplier of foundations for practice may now be seen to support the idea that educational policy should be self-referential. More precisely theoretical institutions may now be seen to legitimize whatever educational policy is proposed by those who happen to have the power to enforce their policy.

As long as educational theory and research are viewed from within an empiricist framework, then it might be reasonably claimed that the institutional arrangements within which much educational theorizing and all teacher training takes place, should continue. Furthermore, as long as these institutional arrangements are assumed by policy-makers and required by their policy then the 'logic' behind those arrangements is likely to reflect the idea that policy guides theory which guides practice. In such a situation it is hardly surprising that some teachers as practitioners should view theory as an unnecessary appendage in a chain of instrumental reasoning in which they seem to be the final link.

Many of those who now work within the colleges and departments of education and who might be expected to be concerned with educational theory, have been left with some combination of the old 'immersing teachers in theory' view of their task or alternatively have assumed the instrumental task of explaining curriculum initiatives to teachers or have devised curriculum support materials for teachers to use. As a result, some colleges and departments have been 'strung along' by the latest curriculum initiative and the latest attempt to find some new form of discourse that is going to act as a standard for all others — for example, the introduction of computing into the curriculum or increasing the 'relevance' of the curriculum or preparing children for work or whatever.

The problems with this instrumental view of educational theory are basically those that I advanced against O'Connor: first, there is the dubious validity of the supposition that there could never be a consensus about educational policy. It is supposed by the proponents of this latest version of instrumentalism that the formulation of policy is outside of logical reasoning. Furthermore, educational policy for such people is not concerned with any empirical testing since empirical testing is supposed by them to be a theoretical matter confined to the measurement of efficiency of method. On this view educational policy is immune from any referents outside itself. It simply directs educational practice and its directives cannot be challenged.

As a result, the idea that theory should guide practice is

supplemented with the idea that policy guides practice. The modest role for theory as supplier of curriculum support materials can only be sustained if it is assumed that curriculum support materials are best produced in isolation from their context of use. However, there seems to be little to support this assumption and plenty to go against it. For example, it is not clear how curriculum materials could be devised without regard to the circumstances in which they might be used. Furthermore, the testing of such materials seems only to be possible in circumstances that best resemble the circumstances in which they will be used. It looks then as if theory drops out of the equation altogether. We might ask what role theoretical institutions, in the form of colleges and departments of education, are to play other than to legitimize educational policy and perhaps to insulate educational policy-makers from the complaints of teachers who might feel that 'things weren't working out too well'.

Second, the problem with this strong sense of 'policy guiding practice' is that it presupposes that both objectives and methods can be precisely specified in advance of the situation to which they will apply. There is also the practical difficulty of knowing just how much detail is required in a policy statement. There is some evidence from attempts at 'centre-periphery' curriculum planning to suggest that policy statements are not a particularly effective way of getting teachers to change their practices.[60] Instead, I suggest in advance of a discussion in Chapter 6 that teachers need to 'make a policy their own' in the sense that their discourse incorporates the evaluative discourse of the policy. That is not to say that whether an utterance is evaluative or descriptive can be decided once and for all. Rather it is to say that the way that teachers use descriptive propositions is in accordance with the way they interpret the evaluative discourse of a policy statement and vice-versa. As Rizvi[61] has argued, the separation of evaluative from descriptive utterances assumed by the proponents of both the policy directing practice view and means-ends curriculum planning, as if utterances could be clearly separated into evaluative or descriptive categories, is a view that we should reject.

Notes and References

1   The debate between D.J. O'CONNOR and P.H. HIRST began in 1957 after the publication of the former's *Introduction to the Philosophy of Education*. The position adopted by O'CONNOR in that publication was still seen by the latter as important enough to warrant extensive mention in his 1983 publication *Educational Theory and its Foundation Disciplines* which was

designed to follow up TIBBLE's (1966) *The Study of Education*. Both books attempted to assess the contributions of the so-called component disciplines to the theory of education.

2 O'CONNOR, D.J. (1973) 'The Nature and Scope of Educational Theory (1)', p. 50.
3 *Ibid.*, p. 52.
4 *Ibid.*, p. 55.
5 *Ibid.*, p. 56.
6 *Ibid.*
7 MILL, J.S. (1859) 'Utilitarianism' in *Utilitarianism, Liberty and Representative Government*.
8 O'CONNOR, D.J., 1973, p. 53.
9 Einstein's first paper on special relativity was 'On the electrodynamics of moving bodies', *Annalen der Physik*, Vol. 17, 1905, pp. 891–921, though this was followed up by several others.
10 O'CONNOR, D.J., 1973, p. 64.
11 *Ibid.*, p. 59.
12 For example GOLBY, M. *et al.* (Eds) (1975) *Curriculum Design*. The chief supporters of 'means–ends' curriculum planning are: BLOOM, B.S. (1956) *Taxonomy of Educational Objectives* in 2 vols, New York, David McKay and Co; MAGER, R.F. (1962) *Preparing Instructional Objectives*, Belmont California, Fearon; TYLER, R. (1950) *Basic Principles of Curriculum and Instruction*, University of Chicago Press; POPHAM, W.J. (1967) *Educational Criterion Measures*, Inglewood California, Southwest Regional Laboratory for Educational Research and Development; DAVIES, I.K. (1975) 'Writing general objectives and writing specific objectives', in GOLBY, M. *et al.*; EISNER, E.W. (1975) 'Instructional and expressive objectives', in GOLBY, M. *et al.* Among the critics of 'means–ends' curriculum planning are: MACDONALD-ROSS, M. (1975) 'Behavioural objectives: A critical review', in Golby, M. *et al.*; PRING, R. (1971) 'Bloom's taxonomy: A philosophical critique (2)', *Cambridge Journal of Education*, 2, pp. 83–91; STENHOUSE, L. (1975) *An Introduction to Curriculum Research and Development*.
13 cf. MALCOLM, N. (1972) *Problems of Mind*.
14 cf. TAYLOR, C. (1979) 'Interpretation and the sciences of man', in his *Philosophical Papers*, 2, 1985.
15 BARROW, R. (1984) *Giving Teaching Back to Teachers*, p. 251.
16 This forms a central part of RIZVI, F. (1983) *The Fact-Value Distinction and the Logic of Educational Theory*.
17 HIRST, P.H. (1974) *Knowledge and the Curriculum*, p. 44.
18 HIRST, P.H., 1983, p. 5.
19 RYLE, G. (1966) *The Concept of Mind*.
20 HIRST, P.H., 1983, p. 5.
21 *Ibid.*, p. 13.
22 Hirst's Forms of Knowledge Thesis has been frequently criticized most recently by Brent, Pring, Evers and Walker. In *Philosophical Foundations for the Curriculum*, 1978, Brent criticizes Hirst for alleged prevarication over the issue of the transcendentalism of the forms. In *Knowledge and Schooling*, 1976, Pring argues that the demarcation criteria between the

forms are inadequate, and in *Epistemology, Semantics and Educational Theory*, 1984, Evers and Walker attempt to highlight logical inconsistencies within Hirst's thesis.

23 HIRST, P.H. and PETERS, R.S. (1970) *The Logic of Education*, p. 6.
24 HARRIS, K. (1979) *Education and Knowledge*, p. 80.
25 WITTGENSTEIN, L. (1979) *Wittgenstein and the Vienna Circle*, p. 113.
26 WITTGENSTEIN, L. (1953) *Philosophical Investigations*, p. 31.
27 *Ibid.*, p. 48.
28 LAKATOS, I. (1978) *Mathematics, Science and Epistemology*, p. 228.
29 HIRST, P.H. and PETERS, R.S., 1970.
30 WITTGENSTEIN, L. (1961) *Tractatus Logico-Philosophicus*.
31 WITTGENSTEIN, L. (1969) *On Certainty*.
32 WITTGENSTEIN, L., 1961, p. 74.
33 EDWARDS, J.C. (1982) *Ethics without Philosophy*.
34 WITTGENSTEIN, L., 1953, p. vii.
35 WITTGENSTEIN, L. (1977) *Culture and Value*, p. 7.
36 *Ibid.*, p. 55.
37 Put simply this means that if someone does not agree with Wittgenstein then they cannot have understood him.
38 For example, LAKATOS, I., 1978, see esp. ch. 11. There he alleges that, in stressing the tacit, Wittgensteinians shift the problem of theory selection on to the problem of selection for membership of an elite. See also GELLNER, E. (1968) *Words and Things*, where he attempts to present Wittgenstein's later philosophy in the form of four theories or 'pillars' in order to criticize followers of Wittgenstein who, Gellner alleges, are opposed to critical examination of their values and ideals. Gellner's main demolition effort is directed against the 'pillar' that the ordinary use of language has normative force. He is able to give many examples where ordinary use is confused and where what common sense tells us turns out to be false. For example, common sense tells us that the earth is flat and that sticks bend when partly immersed in water. Furthermore, he argues that there is no reason why the truth should be presented to us as embodied in ordinary use. Instead, Gellner argues that we have a very powerful method of obtaining truth in science, part of whose method is the clear statement of theses followed by attempts at refutation. By refusing to state their theses clearly, Wittgensteinians seem to be missing what for Gellner is our best method of getting knowledge.
39 Throughout this book I give examples of attempts to reveal the 'tacit' and objectively to clarify the imprecise.
40 Notice that Wittgenstein seems to endorse a 'second order' conception of philosophy when he writes, 'philosophy may in no way interfere with the actual use of language, it can in the end only describe it. For it cannot give it any foundation either. It leaves everything as it is' (1953, p. 49). However, in the context of Wittgenstein's other writing, the phrase 'it leaves everything as it is' occupies a different role from the language game of doing nothing. Instead it points to a role for the philosopher as 'shower', the maker of a selection of perspicuous representations that represent the world in a different way. G.E. MOORE reported 'that what he, Wittgenstein, had at "the back of his mind" was

"the idea that aesthetic discussions were like discussions in a court of law" where one tries to "clear up the circumstances of the action" which is being tried, hoping that in the end what one says will "appeal to the judge". And he said that the same sort of "reasons" were given, not only in Ethics, but also in Philosophy' (*Philosophical Papers*, 1959, p. 315)

41 LOCKE, J. (1690) *An Essay Concerning Human Understanding*, referred to here in the Woozley edition, Collins, 1964, p. 58.
42 *Ibid.*
43 ASPIN, D.N. (1982) 'Philosophy of Education', p. 11.
44 *Ibid.*, p. 12.
45 The famous 'cogito ergo sum' put forward in the *Discourse on Method* by DESCARTES, R., 1912, now in many editions.
46 *Ibid.*, p. 28.
47 WITTGENSTEIN, L. (1977) *On Certainty*.
48 WITTGENSTEIN, L. (1953) *Philosophical Investigations*, pp. 92–5. The discussion of 'Sensation S' merges into a discussion of 'pain'. Wittgenstein tries to imagine the case where someone writes 'S' in a diary every time that he experiences a particular sensation. Wittgenstein attempts to show that such a performance is meaningless unless it is sometimes accompanied by some other change in behaviour which is a recognized part of our 'form of life' so that someone else might be able to check the occurrence of the sensation by asking questions like 'what do you feel?', 'is it a permanent sensation?' and so on.
49 HOLLAND, R.F. (1980) *Against Empiricism*, p. 10.
50 M. BODEN discusses some of these in her *Artificial Intelligence and Natural Man*, 1977.
51 PAPERT, S. (1980) *Mindstorms: Children, Computers, and Powerful Ideas*.
52 PUTNAM, H. (1978) *Meaning and the Moral Sciences*, p. 57, reports that 'several million dollars and many man hours of bright people's time was spent on ... the project of making explicit the constraints involved in translation ... Result essentially complete failure'.
53 DEARDEN, R.F. (1984) *Theory and Practice in Education*, p. 4.
54 *Ibid.* See also LLOYD, D.I. (1976) 'Theory and Practice', p. 98.
55 WILSON, J. (1972) *Philosophy and Educational Research*.
56 *Ibid.*, p. 13.
57 WILSON, J. (1982) 'The credibility of educational studies', *Oxford Review of Education*, 8, pp. 3–19.
58 See PETERS, R.S. (1966) *Ethics and Education*, pp. 46–91, for his account of the idea of 'education as initiation'. This is the idea that education should consist of an initiation into the 'forms of Knowledge'.
59 There are many examples of this kind of analysis in *The International Library of the Philosophy of Education*, general editor R.S. PETERS, publisher Routledge and Kegan Paul. For example; DEARDEN, R.F., HIRST, P.H. and PETERS, R.S. (Eds) (1972) *Education and the Development of Reason*; SNOOK, I.A. (Ed.) (1972) *Concepts of Indoctrination*; PETERS, R.S. (Ed.) (1967) *The Concept of Education*.
60 STENHOUSE, L. (1975) *An Introduction to Curriculum Development*, p. 218.
61 RIZVI, F. (1983) *The Fact-Value Distinction and the Logic of Educational Theory*.

Chapter 2

Practical Implications

The previous chapter was concerned to claim that APE and O'Connor's account of educational theory reinforce each other within a common epistemology — that of foundationalist empiricism — and how that epistemology can be seen to underpin the presently common view that educational theorists should be concerned with maximizing the efficiency of means to the exclusion of debate about those ends and values to which the means are supposed to be directed. In this chapter I argue that an adherence to this epistemology also lies behind those attitudes and values that have structured and directed some recent curricular and administrative recommendations. I go on to claim that many of these recommendations are educationally undesirable.

Such attitudes and values may be characterized by what I call 'objectivism'. An 'objectivist' might be supposed to support the kind of recommendations against which I shall strongly inveigh. Empiricist foundationalist epistemology underpins objectivism through the idea that beliefs can be justified by a chain of reasons that end in a foundation of certainty and the further idea that researchers may elucidate this chain of reasons in order to substantiate claims to knowledge.

While I investigate the educational implications of objectivism under separate headings, the degree of overlap between the ideas of vocationalism, consumerism, managerialism and objectivism may be taken as an indication of their mutual coherence. I conclude with an imaginary example of a curriculum initiative that might serve further to illustrate the extent of this coherence.

Vocationalism

It is commonly accepted that the natural sciences are responsible for an increase in the material well-being of those societies that support scientific endeavour. Some social scientists argue that this material well-being could be increased further if the social sciences were able to emulate the natural sciences and if members of a society were to give up something of their sense of community and free-will in favour of their being willing to be regarded as 'objects' to which causal generalizations would be appropriate. For example, Gellner suggests that members of a society might agree to run their public institutions on instrumental lines in order to have increased private freedom. He advocates

> a pluralist affluent society, in which people are free, economically and politically, to pursue their romantic fulfilment at home, while in the public sphere good instrumental institutions prevent tyranny and watch over the overall economic performance ... What on earth is wrong with having one's expression at home (paperback classics, hi-fi) and leaving the public sphere to soulless pragmatism?[1]

The educational consequence of this compromise may be seen to be reflected in the dichotomy between vocational and academic education, about which some industrialists and businessmen complain. It is as if vocational education should be concerned with preparing people for a purely instrumental role at work whereas an academic education should be concerned with the development of people's ability to express themselves 'at home'. O'Connor puts forward a variant of this view when he argues that

> What is needed, both at school level and in higher education is a large-scale switch to the study of natural science and mathematics.... (As for the humanities) for those with a natural affinity for them, a minimal amount of elementary schooling will put them in a position to enjoy them if they wish to.[2]

In line with the compromise suggested by Gellner, O'Connor bases his argument on a distinction between an essential body of basic knowledge and techniques which are necessary for the efficient running of society ... and ... a wider body of skills and attitudes which encompass ... what journalists would call 'the cultural heritage of mankind'.[3]

Recently governments on both sides of the Atlantic have presented an economic argument making a similar case for a large-scale switch to vocational studies. This argument has become so dominant in current educational debate that much curriculum development is presently concerned with the making and implementation of such a switch.[4] The empiricist idea that 'theory guides practice' is central to the making of such a switch. For example, in the case of teacher training, trainees are prepared for their future role as teachers by some sort of structured immersion into those things that the colleges and departments deem as appropriate guides to the practice of teaching. Similarly an objectivist might assume that workers generally may be prepared for their future occupations by a structured immersion into those 'theories' that are presented in schools and 'vocational' colleges.

In Britain, vocational further education has recently been given much prominence through the incursion of the Manpower Services Commission (MSC) (now called the Training Commission) into the realm that was previously reserved for the Department of Education and Science and the Scottish Education Department.[5] Schemes like the Technical and Vocational Educational Initiative (TVEI), the Continuing Provision of Vocational Education (CPVE), the extension of the Youth Training Scheme (YTS), the Action Plan and the recent Review of Vocational Qualifications (RVQ) leading to the setting-up of the National Council for Vocational Qualifications (NCVQ) embody some of the recent moves towards what I call vocationalism in education.

The colleges of further education in Britain and the vocational and technical schools in the USA have never been in much doubt about their central role as providers of vocational education.[6] Increasingly, too, American community colleges are developing 'prevocational' curricula following the recommendations of the Carnegie Report.[7] Paradoxically, however, these colleges and schools have expanded as employment opportunities have decreased. Throughout this expansion, vocational education may be seen to have been concerned with the set of theories that are supposed to guide vocational practice whether their client group was predominantly unemployed or employed.[8] Yet it might be reasonably maintained that, even in the hey-day of low unemployment, the instruction given in vocational colleges was often divorced from the realities of industrial life. For example, Gleeson and Mardle write:

> For the apprentice-student, the shop floor represents the real basis of his material existence. College represents an escape route, a ladder to potential promotion and higher wages. It is also seen to be a 'perk', a day off from industrial reality.[9]

Research on the role and concept of further education is not extensive, but the plethora of curriculum initiatives with which further education has had to grapple over the past thirty years or so[10] might be taken to support the contention that the sort of instruction which young people get in their colleges does not easily match industrial reality — and merely serves as a sort of hurdle which workers must overcome in order to gain promotion or even a job! This doubt about the general effectiveness of vocational education was echoed by the Carnegie Council in the USA[11] which reported that

> Among male youth with identical years of schooling (for example, 12) those who have had school-based occupational training are, on the average, no better off and no worse off in terms of unemployment experience, rate of pay, or job satisfaction than those who pursued general or academic studies.[12]

Oakeshott's work might be used to explain the lack of relevance of some of the instruction offered in institutions of vocational education. Oakeshott points out that technical knowledge, which he defines as knowledge of technique that can be formulated in rules, gets its moment of application in practical knowledge, which he defines as traditional knowledge that exists only in use. For example, to become a joiner involves much more than learning a series of techniques in abstraction from their actual applications in the sort of work that joiners do. Hence Oakeshott mourns the advance of the idea that technical knowledge could be taught in abstraction from the community of practitioners who sustain the discourse with which an apprentice is supposed to become familiar. As he puts it:

> Apprenticeship, the pupil working alongside the master who in teaching a technique also imparts the sort of knowledge that cannot be taught, has not yet disappeared; but it is obsolescent, and its place is being taken by technical schools.[13]

Consequently, for Oakeshott, the move supposedly to maximize efficiency of learning by teaching technical knowledge in colleges in abstraction from and as a preparation for work, can never replace the sort of learning that comes with working alongside someone with the aim of being inducted into a practice. For Oakeshott direct experience is everything in this kind of learning.

As unemployment began to rise in Britain, the dominance of objectivism that lay behind some of the attitudes and values of those who designed the further education curriculum might be seen to be responsible for the lack of debate about whether people could be prepared for particular types of work. The assumption continued that colleges of further education should attend to the development of vocational preparation curricula. For example, it is argued on behalf of the Manpower Services Commission[14] that unemployment may be partly attributable to a mismatch between the competences that the unemployed presently have and the competences that the unemployed would need to have in order to do those jobs that are available. Hence the MSC encourages the colleges of further education to provide short vocational preparation 'update'[15] courses in order to satisfy the supply side of the unemployment equation. The difficulty for the colleges comes when deciding what the content of such courses should be.

The colleges of further education may be seen to have been founded on the empiricist idea that theory guides practice but as they became sensitive to the possibility that such theory did not appear to be readily available, the emphasis shifted and the key idea seems to have become 'transferable skills and competences'.[16] Now part of the reasoning behind this shift may well have been due to the belief that people who did not appear to be good at writing or 'academic' study often seemed good at doing practical things. Some curriculum designers may not have taken into account that this might be a case of wants (in the sense that learners are often prompted by the desire for some success) replacing needs (and these may have been shown up by failure to 'cotton on' at the first attempt). These designers began to downgrade technical knowledge and proclaimed vocational skills and competences to be the new foundations for rational practice.

The paradox is that empiricism provides the rationale for this move by suggesting that all investigation should begin anew and that knowledge is only obtained when the mind is continually being cleared of 'prejudice'[17] — to the extent that subject knowledge is said to become outdated so quickly that the learning of content does not matter so much as the learning of processes. At that point curricular experts of the empiricist persuasion started looking at what they claimed to be the basic processes of learning. It was argued that since subject knowledge becomes outdated so quickly, it is preferable to teach the process whereby knowledge is obtained. Unfortunately these experts fail to see that they are involved in a regress here. Logically the regress can only be avoided by denying the empiricist theory that lies behind the experts' attitudes and values.

However, as a matter of fact, these experts attempt to halt this regress through the notion of a learning process. For example, if it is agreed that there is no value in someone's concern to learn to know that the Second World War ended in 1945, because 'facts' can be obtained from a computerized data-base, then it will seem to make sense to teach people to use a computerized data-base; the use of a computerized data-base can be learnt by consulting a manual, so it makes more sense to know how to get hold of and to interpret a manual; this in turn leads to — and so on. The problem that faces the expert is to decide the exact point at which to break in to the regress. A variety of suggestions have been tried. For example, in many countries the ideas of context-free competences, of skills that are independent of content[18] have gained in importance. However, having considered many of these ideas, the OECD reported that

> it is difficult to find ways of turning abstract conceptions such as transfer, learning to learn, or general problem-solving, into concrete operations.[19]

In Britain, the idea of an 'occupational training family' (OTF) of various skills and competences has been developed at great length and expense.[20] Let us unravel these terms as they apply to the Youth Training Scheme (YTS). The designers of this scheme claim that it is possible to describe 103 'skills' that are generic and transferable and which in various combinations can be mastered in order to prepare people, not just for one job, but for a range of jobs. There is no room here to examine what might be meant by 'life-skills', 'social skills', 'survival skills' and 'coping skills' or to elucidate the differences between them.[21] Suffice to say that the designers of such curricular recommendations feel able to group these and other skills into eleven occupational training families (OTF) of skills and competences that are supposed to prepare people for jobs within those families.[22]

The designers of YTS schemes, however, go further than this in proposing that there should be 'transfer learning objectives' (TLO)[23] set for YTS trainees, the achievement of which is supposed to enable them to find work in another OTF should that prove necessary. Hence, while trainees are supposed to be mastering those skills and competences appropriate to a particular OTF, they are also supposed to be achieving some TLOs in order to be flexible enough to meet future demands of the labour market. However, essentially the function of the TLO seems to involve closing up a division that was only opened by the eleven-fold classification of occupations into OTFs.

To take Jonathan's example[24] the occupations of cobbler, electrician, garage mechanic and window cleaner are grouped within OTF4 (installation, maintenance and repair occupations). Now it is difficult to see what common features there are between the skills and competences involved in doing the work of a cobbler and a window-cleaner over and above those that might relate to a cobbler and a vending machine operator (to take an example from OTF8). It is difficult to support the idea that skills, competences and even knowledge float free of their moment of application in the concrete tasks and in the particular vocational contexts in which cobblers, vending machine operatives and others operate.

It is not surprising that those concerned with the design and policy of the YTS should leave the matter of the content of YTS programmes to the work of individual sponsors and training agencies, aided by publications from bodies such as the FEU[25] that suggest how the notions of context free competences might be achieved. The problem with the implementation of these suggestions, as Jonathan[26] notes, is that the trainee might end up stocking supermarket shelves while the trainer ticks off the competences supposedly 'overcome' on a checklist — competences such as 'plan the order of activities', 'decide which category something belongs in'. These competences might be worth acquiring if they represented something new and valuable to the trainee; however, when applied to stocking supermarket shelves, it is likely that the trainee will have achieved as much in the way of exhibiting mastery of such examples of those competences in the course of travelling to the supermarket in the morning. Of course stocking supermarket shelves is an extremely useful activity. What is dangerous is the elevation of such an activity to the status of something that is regarded as having the power somehow to prepare the trainee for a range of occupations, should supermarket jobs not materialize, and moreover that pretends that such an activity is necessarily educational in character.

Perhaps the move to OTFs and competences is as far as the empiricist 'theory guiding practice' idea will get; perhaps the thrust into vocationalism may be seen to result from the fragmentation of practical discourse into elements that seemed able to provide a political *rationale* for learning but did little to offer a different kind of educational value for the lives of those who were deemed to have become competent in OTFs and TLOs. I am not arguing that all forms of vocational education should be abandoned. Nor am I arguing that the only worthwhile form of learning is by practice in context. To argue thus would be as silly as arguing, for example, that all instruction in bricklaying must take place in the rain because it often rains while bricklayers work! It may well be the case that a short preparation for specific vocations within colleges suits both employers, trainees and government. However, if the above argument is correct, this cannot just be assumed nor especially can it be assumed that a general vocational preparation is either possible or desirable.

Consumerism

The central difficulty with empiricism is that it seems to leave the determination of desirable ends either to the vagaries of public interest or to political, social or moral norms that are impossible to quantify. However, the idea that educational value can be instrumentally assessed according to economic criteria seems to offer the possibility of an objective determination of educational aims. I follow an argument of Gellner in order to explain how this possibility might have arisen.

Gellner argues that western capitalist democracies in the nineteenth and twentieth centuries may be characterized by the way in which a minority has exploited a large majority with no means of sustaining that exploitation other than through the idea of a 'Danegeld state' which guarantees

> a steady spread of affluence, and the expectation — for the first time in history — of *continuous* improvement ... The expansion was oiled by a gradual inflation of the currency ... egalitarianism in education, and so forth. A regular and expected growth in income, social security and governmental responsibility for employment, constitute a permanent and growing bribe by means of which the system could purchase acquiescence from those who were not its most privileged beneficiaries.[27] (original emphasis)

In the 1970s, however, the supply of Danegeld started to dry up. Armed with neither carrot nor stick, what Gellner calls 'the system' had to look to other things to sustain itself. Three elements seem to me to be implied in this search. First, the success of a political appeal to the conservatism of the working class; second, attempts to suggest that one or other aspect of the welfare state is primarily responsible for the present lack of Danegeld. Public education seems to be an ideal candidate for such a charge. For if it is assumed that public education forms the closed system necessary to support a utilitarian idea of maximizing efficiency, then it becomes easy to blame the public education system for its inability to produce the sort and number of citizens needed to maintain the finance which keeps the system running. Moreover, the state education system itself requires considerable finance, thus reducing the amount available for everything else. Hence the state education system is seen to be worthy of censure on two counts. The third element is the various attempts to distribute finan cial rewards more fairly and thus to gain some sort of moral currency through a 'legitimacy of distribution'. According to Gellner[28] there are two possible ways that an industrial society may legitimately distribute the benefits at its disposal: either the so-called 'free market' or Marxism. Gellner speedily dismisses the Marxist option and concentrates on the idea of a 'market'. As he puts it:

> men have needs and desires, and work so as to satisfy these. Their productivity grows immensely through the division of labour and specialization. This in turn raises the question of the terms on which mutually complementary producers exchange their products. A 'free market' is best: it stimulates further endeavour into production of those goods which 'at the margin' still give most satisfaction. The market price, if not warped by interference, is not merely the one leading to the best utilisation of effort, but also constitutes a fair and legitimate price.[29]

Plainly the idea of a 'market' is the dominant model for such a distribution in the 1980s. As Gellner notes, the idea of a 'market' appears to offer the final foundation for empiricism in that this idea places

> the burden of decision to something empirical, testable, observable — namely observable preferences, demand and supply.[30]

The 'market' acts as a kind of neutral arbiter between competing interests that can be used to settle matters in a way that meets the objectivist's criterion for quantification of value according to how much people are prepared to spend to get what they want. However, there are at least four difficulties with the notion of distribution according to the 'market': first, the 'market' only gives its verdict in an institutional and cultural context that is made and manipulated by men. Second, industrial production is inseparable from an infrastructure the depth and extent of which makes it absurd to suppose that the contributions of individuals can be separated out. Third, wants are not the same as needs and it is neither unreasonable nor improper that government should intervene in order to secure some longer term objectives against those which might be dictated by some of the short-term demands of the 'market'. Finally, and most importantly, if government has to intervene, then the fruits of its intervention, far from presenting fresh challenges and opportunities, merely present opportunities for early exploitation of government decisions. That is to say, those who have early information about possible or likely consequences are most likely to do well out of a decision. This has been apparent most recently in the case of government decisions to privatize nationalized industries but also becomes apparent in the case of decisions to close schools and to increase support for private education. For example, if a decision is taken to close what is widely regarded as a good school within the public sector on the grounds that its catchment area is too small and if it is proposed that pupils should be sent to what is widely regarded as a poor school, then however valid those evaluations might be, a parent who receives early information about the closure plans would be likely to benfit by moving home before a glut of property appears on the housing market due to increased numbers of parents in search of another good school.[31]

The real difficulty with adopting the idea of a 'free-market' as neutral arbiter, is that people come to see through what might in reality be an illusion and the attempt to legitimate distribution is lost. Hence not only does self-interest become channelled to subvert the system but also 'ideal conviction' is set to join forces with it. Gellner suggests that while the market might be an excellent way of carrying out minor adjustments to the pattern of distribution, there is no substitute for political responsibility in the overall economic sphere. Recent government debates within Britain about 'educational vouchers' and action to privatize the further education sector and to switch funding from institution-led courses to consumer-led courses (where the Training Commission is assumed to represent the consumer) seem to support the view that the present government in the UK operates on the model of dictating the patterns of direction and growth in education via market forces. In North America, too, it seems that successive conservative administrations have invoked the notion of 'market forces' to justify their educational policies.[32]

If the market is to be the final arbiter of educational worth, then logically there needs to be a commodity which can be marketed. In education this 'commodity' appears to be knowledge. Now empiricist epistemology supports the idea that knowledge consists in bundles of statements that somehow match the world; on this model educational institutions can offer the learner the opportunity to get hold of different combinations of these bundles of statements in the form of 'units of study' or 'modules'. It is not hard to find evidence to support the view that the 1970s and 1980s have seen a great increase in the numbers of courses, modules and units conceived along these lines that have been produced across the educational spectrum[33] suggesting a kind of 'assembly-line' notion of knowledge.

However, we might wonder on what basis the learner is to make the choice between or among such units. Very often the answer appears to be on the basis of the jobs that are thought to be likely to be on offer. In other words, the supposed availability of certain types of job appears to be the ultimate arbiter in the choice of what is worth studying — vocationalism and consumerism are partners in educational policy. Now no one would blame parents for considering that this is a useful way of viewing what some educational provision should be about. Few parents want to see their offspring spending their post-school years unemployed. However, such an overall view of the function and utility of educational institutions is open to question on at least four counts.

First, we can often only have a vague idea about what jobs in future, if any, there might be; it seems to make little sense to direct our whole educational effort towards preparing people for jobs that can only be speculatively envisaged. Since educational output can never match employment demand precisely, there might always be some residual disappointment of expectation. At worst a vocational bias can amount to little more than a crude form of social engineering that may well be likely to fail. Furthermore, the problem with a conception of learning that relies upon precise specifications of input and output is that there is little scope for encompassing the idea of the learner's being able to continue with something on his own and moreover to be able to do more than just one set of things — namely those skills etc. described or looked for in a job specification.

Second, failure to achieve vocational targets could easily lead to the opposite reaction, that is towards the idea that education should be directed at whatever children were interested in, as if children were somehow apart from the society which they are supposed to join. In other words, when the curriculum is based on objectivist presuppositions regarding what might be called 'pre-vocationalism' — and when 'pre-vocationalism' is seen to fail, there is the possibility of a lurching towards the opposite idea of an extreme form of liberalism. (It may be that the present move towards 'pre-vocationalism' is itself the result of a lurching in the opposite direction away from the liberal curricular ideas of the 1960s.) However, people not only want to earn their living but also want to play some part in determining the way a society might develop; and that seems for us to mean our being able to criticize existing institutions while still contributing to them. We need to rebuild our boat while still remaining afloat, to use an analogy borrowed from Neurath. No one can totally jettison the society of which they are a part, any more than anyone can totally shape the society which they want to join.

Third, the idea of the market as ultimate arbiter ignores the fact that people also care about what they do and how they do it, not just the material rewards that their work brings. Were everybody to be totally concerned with material reward and were the utilitarian separation of work from leisure to be accepted, then we should end up having to apportion wealth on the basis of misery endured at work; and while there may be some need to reward people for doing unpleasant or dangerous work, that is no reason to suppose that such an apportionment could ever form the basis of an equitable incomes policy or fair basis for any kind of distribution of social goods or wealth. If it did, then there would be a tendency for people to make their particular occupation appear far more miserable than it actually was!

Fourth, even if these difficulties with instrumental assessments of value are ignored, the objectivist still faces the problem of devising the most efficient ways of acquiring knowledge and assessing how effectively it has been acquired. These tasks might appear to the objectivist to be the preserve of the colleges and departments of education who might be assigned the task of devising curricular experiments, the aim of which would be to produce curriculum support materials that maximize 'efficiency' where efficiency is defined as the inverse of the cost of each student taking a unit of study. The so-called 'Information Technology' revolution is seen by many[34] to offer great possibilities here, for, if it is assumed that knowledge is readily available 'at the touch of a button' as it were, then educationalists can concentrate on the technical matter of getting the appropriate equipment into the right places and in a format suitable for people with differing levels of abilities.

The economic advantages of such a system arise out of the assumed reduction in the number of teachers and in the remuneration that is paid to them, for if some sort of elite group of educationalists could devise the software to run on such equipment, educational institutions could be staffed by technicians (perhaps called teachers). The claim that educational technicians should, in such a system, be paid substantially more than other types of technician could hardly be substantiated. Such a system, furthermore, would seem to offer the possibility of measuring teacher effectiveness, for if input and output can be measured and curricular method is assumed to be standardized, then any failure to achieve targets of cost efficiency can only be attributable to the inefficiency of the teacher.

While this scenario may be bleak and while few teachers might wish to contemplate its implementation, it may be seen as the logical conclusion to objectivistic ideas about education. We may summarize these ideas as follows: educational values are supposed to be determined by appeals to the amount of money that people are prepared to spend to achieve them and can thus be determined mathematically, as can the selection of educational means by equating cost per 'bit' of knowledge acquired — with efficiency.[35]

In conclusion, it appears as if the idea that the market can provide a neutral arbiter in determining educational value is a myth. One danger with perpetrating this myth is that educational values are seen to be relativistic. On this view educational theorists seem obliged to try to secure the patronage of those who happen to have the power to manage educational change. As I shall argue, the notion of managerialism is predicated upon the same objectivistic presuppositions that underpin consumerism. Hence there is the possibility that current educational theory and practice are underpinned by a particular set of values and that only those who can easily subscribe to those values are likely to be able to work comfortably within the education system. Unfortunately as I mentioned earlier, many teachers and others find it increasingly difficult to experience this comfort, yet the dominance of objectivism works against the promotion of a more open and democratic education system.

Managerialism

It has recently been suggested in many places that the lack of good management in educational institutions is responsible for many of the deficiencies in the state education system. A typical example is provided by the *Report into the Pay and Conditions of Service of School Teachers in Scotland*.[36] In that document it is suggested that education is something that can be 'managed', in the sense that the overall aims of education can be determined by appeals to 'market demands' and that these aims can be broken down into objectives that specify target outputs in relation to inputs and for which 'managers' can be responsible. As I have argued, however, the market — and especially that for education — does not give its verdict in a way that makes it obvious what individuals should do in order to contribute to the satisfaction of 'market demands'. Instead, there is a need to interpret the market and to subdivide that interpretation into objectives that teachers and others should aspire to achieve. These objectives may then be operationalized and, through a chain or 'line' structure, the market is supposed to be satisfied by various line managers achieving their targets predicated upon those objectives and their operationalizations.

In Britain, we have seen many examples of this type of educational managerialism in the past few years. These examples are easily recognizable by the new titles that have been assumed by some people who occupy positions at the top of educational hierarchies. For example, we find heads of schools and colleges referring to themselves as senior managers. Some polytechnic principals refer to themselves as chief executives and at the other end of the hierarchy we find teachers referred to as 'MPGs', which is often short for 'main professional grades' though could easily be shortened still further to 'operatives' or 'Os'!

Now the very real problem that faces those who attempt to make what I have called managerialism work in education is that it is not obvious just what the inputs and outputs to the education system are. Plainly the input consists partly of finance and the output consists partly of overall economic prosperity, yet we do not have a formula or model by which these two can be related, let alone measured. Nor do we have a means of measuring what MacIntyre calls 'internal goods' that may well be the most important parts of educational transactions. Accuracy, style and most of all perhaps commitment are examples of 'goods' that are internal to teaching and

which cannot be had in any other way ... nor ... identified
and recognised [other than] by the experience of participating
in the practice in question.

Of course our new educational 'managers' strive to develop so-called
'performance indicators' and the means of weighing one such indicator against another so that 'internal goods' might be objectified. Yet as
MacIntyre points out, the attempt to objectify 'internal goods' may
destroy them.

MacIntyre distinguishes between institutions and practices in
order to draw our attention to the way that managers might be
considered to be concerned principally with institutions whereas
teaching might be viewed as a practice. Now while I do not believe
that this distinction can be drawn as sharply as MacIntyre seems to
suppose, I do believe that MacIntyre is right to notice that managers
are characteristically concerned with things like power, status and
money which he calls 'external goods' and which sustain institutions.
MacIntyre is also right to notice that there is a tension between the
manager's competitive search for external goods and teachers own
attempts to realize internal goods.

[T]he ideals and creativity of the practice are always vulnerable
to the ... competitiveness of the institution.

Hence managers have the power to corrupt the sense of community
among teachers necessary for the successful flourishing of a practice.

MacIntyre draws our attention to the important point that the
attempt to managerialize education is not simply a methodological
device to improve the basis on which educational decisions might be
made, rather it is itself evaluative and likely to corrupt the sense of
mutual support that many teachers develop as an essential aid to their
professional practice. This point may be illustrated by considering
three motivational methods that appear to be available and used by
managers. First, there is extrinsic motivation such as is provided by
some combination of the 'carrot and stick' method; second, there is
intrinsic motivation that depends upon the coincidence of target
objectives with those things that the manager or workforce value for
their own sake, rather than for the sake of some perceived external
benefit; and third, there is an ultimate appeal to the idea that the
'common good' can be satisfied if individual desires are suspended in

favour of externally set targets which are determined ultimately by an appeal to the market.

There is no room here to debate at length whether the 'common good' can be satisfied in this way. I have already indicated some of the logical inadequacies with the thesis that educational aims can be determined exclusively by an appeal to what consumers want. It is worth, however, supplementing my earlier argument here by pointing out that it is by no means clear who the consumers of education are. Students, parents, industrialists and others all may claim to use the education service but may make differing demands upon it. It is also not clear that an untrammelled appeal to what might be called 'consumerism' in education is compatible with the orderly administration of the education system. Nor is it clear that such an appeal can avoid giving rise to what would widely be regarded as an unacceptable difference between the quality of the educational provision demanded by one set of articulate and vocal consumers and the quality of the educational provision demanded by or perhaps provided for their less articulate counterparts. On the other hand, it has to be recognized that the present British system whereby teachers and individual local education authorities decide much of what goes on in those parts of the education system over which they exercise some control, is no longer acceptable to many people.

We have here an opposition between two views that might be called 'consumerism' and 'professionalism' with apparently no way to settle matters other than to appeal to whatever norms are politically acceptable. For the moment that means 'consumerism', as is shown by the present British Government's endorsement of the Report mentioned above. The industrial action that followed publication of that Report, however, may be taken as an indication that many teachers do not believe that the 'common good' will be satisfied by instituting a consumer-related view of education administered by a system of 'line managers'. Whether teachers are correct in this belief is irrelevant to my argument. It is relevant, however, that only intrinsic and extrinsic motivational methods appear to be available to encourage teachers to accept the strengthening of line management in schools so that the aims of education, as set by the 'consumers', might be realized.

In the case of teaching, potentially at any rate, intrinsic motivation seems high as a logical justification. However, recently there has been a move to increase the element of extrinsic motivation for teachers[37] perhaps as a compensation for the loss of intrinsic motivation that is often quoted as having occurred.[38] It can be argued, however, that recent moves towards instituting a line-management system or structure of procedures in educational institutions emanate not only as responses to the demand for 'accountability' to 'consumers' but also from an attempt to increase the number of means of motivating teachers extrinsically. I shall argue that such a notion of a 'management structure' is manipulative because the idea of objectivity assumed within the structure is bogus. The imposition of a line-management structure not only gives rise to the dubious proposition that teachers can be rewarded according to the extent to which they achieve target objectives but also to the fiction that there is such a thing as managerial expertise — either generally or in education. In short, I shall argue that the idea of line-management is inappropriate in an educational context.

For extrinsic motivation to be effective in the case of teachers, at least two conditions must be met. First, there must be some way of fairly rewarding teachers for their performance; this seems to mean that performance must be measured in terms of 'output' over 'input' for that part of the educational system for which the teacher is responsible. Second, the individual teacher's effort needs to be isolated from other influences. There are good reasons to suppose that neither condition can be met.

In the first case students are remarkably variable, such that we do not have any reliable means of measuring their capabilities. External examinations have often been regarded as the most appropriate or even the best psychometric device for such purposes, but they are unreliable and have notoriously low predictive validity. In the second case it is doubtful whether an individual teacher's effort can be isolated from all other factors. Not only do some decisions have to be taken collectively within a school — things like room changes and disciplinary matters — but also some decisions that radically affect a teacher's performance depend upon the decisions of those who are paid to manage him; an example would refer to things like timetabling, provision of resources, class sizes and so on. Moreover, the total educational experience is not isolatable from other influences on people's lives — television, magazines and so on. In short, a hard empiricist's condition for objective measurement of teacher performance cannot be met.

An objectivist, on the other hand, might suggest that the manager's interpretation of the market provides the permanent foundations for evaluative theory. In order to justify that interpretation, managers have to make it look as if their judgments were based on some impersonal criterion. Yet such a criterion must be a fiction for, apart from the market, there is no other appeal to objectivity. For the objectivist of this persuasion, judgmental criteria come from the market-place or not at all.

This is the import of one of MacIntyre's arguments in *After Virtue*.[39] According to MacIntyre, means-ends rationality necessarily embodies the idea of manipulative social relations in which moral argument consists of veiled expressions of preference. This is termed 'emotivism' by MacIntyre and is said to lead to 'the obliteration of any genuine distinction between manipulative and non-manipulative social relations'.[40]

The only way that managers might avoid this conclusion is to base their decisions on those observations that can be intersubjectively validated. However, this move shifts the emphasis over to those things that are indirectly concerned with student learning, for example curriculum development and administration. The danger is that these observable parts of a teacher's responsibility become the sole measure of the extent to which teachers should be rewarded. This is particularly the case when schools have to face a steady barrage of curriculum initiatives that need to be interpreted, resources that need to be pre-pared and a plethora of administrative tasks that need to be carried out, in order to demonstrate that such initiatives are being imple-mented according to some other set of management objectives exter-nally imposed upon them.

The pressure on managers is to reward those who most contri-bute to such publicly observable identifiable outcomes at the expense of those who only concentrate on their own teaching. However, the latter group might not merely feel discontent because of a downgrad-ing of what they perceive to be the most important part of their job but their discontent might be increased when they realize that their expertise is not such a significant factor when it comes to the way in which managers apportion the rewards accruing to the institution by means of promotions and so on. If classroom teaching commands such a low status that the only hope for a career teacher of gaining rewards is to be promoted out of the classroom and out of the way of implementing curricular developments that seem to involve attempts to prepare people for a future that none of us can predict with any great accuracy, it is paradoxical that the most likely motivation for teachers seriously working on such developments is the possibility of promotion as a reward for involvement in them. It is hardly surpris-ing then that morale among many teachers is reported to be extremely low.[41]

It should be noted that this argument against the idea of a 'line-management' structure in educational institutions does not carry with it the implication that a structure of promoted posts is inappropriate in an educational context, merely that such a structure cannot be straight-forwardly assumed to be appropriate for education on the basis of its alleged or supposed applicability in other contexts in which more sense can be made of the idea of intersubjectively verifiable target outputs. Instead some other justification is required. I reconsider this issue in Chapter 6.

An Imaginary Example of Curriculum Development

We have seen how foundationalist empiricist epistemology coheres with a particular set of educational practices and ideas. Let me now summarize the extent of this coherence by setting out some of the features that we might expect an imaginary curriculum initiative to display if I am correct in arguing that empiricist foundationalist epistemology dominates current educational policy-making. I expect that most readers will be able to recognize similarities between particular curricular developments with which they are familiar and the imaginary one that I present below.

The curriculum initiative might be announced in a consultative paper that described a situation of poor economic performance within the host country coupled with unfavourable international comparisons of participation rates in vocational education. It might be claimed that old vocational qualifications were not widely understood nor accepted and that people were not being prepared adequately for working life. It may also be claimed that the school curriculum is ineffective because young people are not interested in it, with the corollary that if the school curriculum were more vocational then more young people would be motivated to learn. There would be little mention of other possible causes of lack of motivation, such as a dissatisfaction with the society and its institutions which students are supposed to be prepared to join, a realistic appraisal of the employment opportunities, or a feeling that there is something gravely mistaken about such a view of education anyway.

Thus we might identify many empiricist assumptions in this consultative paper — the separation of the vocational from the academic, the idea of a vocational preparation, the idea that a general education may well be a 'waste of time' and the idea that young people are and should be primarily interested in preparing for a particular occupation with the corollary that the nature of such a preparation is relatively unproblematic. Finally, we might not expect to be invited to comment on the validity of these assumptions. By limiting the enquiry in this way, the framework for policy making would have been set. A respondent would either reinforce the framework or give answers deemed irrelevant. The framework for policy making would be self-referential and coherent with a type of theorizing that an empiricist might endorse.

The initiative itself would probably be announced with a flourish as if all other efforts to educate had been deeply mistaken — words like exciting, innovative and challenging would probably be used and it might be claimed that everybody agrees that there is a clear need for reform. The main thrust of this reform would be to modularize or unitize courses of study so that curricular provision would be flexible and responsive to regular updating. Employers would be encouraged to involve themselves in the design of these modules or units and educationalists would be encouraged to prepare suitable teaching materials or packages through which students could work at their own pace in an 'open' format. Teachers would then be encouraged to become 'student-centred' and 'manage' the classroom as technicians so that students work through packages as efficiently as possible. Thus this innovation would follow what I earlier described as the centralist strategy of 'policy guiding practice' and theorists would be left with two possible roles. Either they could devise and coordinate curriculum support materials or they may simply legitimize the curriculum initiative itself by explaining it to teachers during in-service training sessions or by doing curriculum development work under the guise of research.

I have tried to show via this imaginary example that the present dominance of foundationalist empiricism within education coheres with the view that policy matters cannot be justified with arguments that go beyond appeals to economic considerations, to majority public interest or to political/social/moral norms. As a result, consultations about policy are necessarily limited. There is no theoretical apparatus for combining or settling a variety of contributions from a variety of perspectives if they conflict. The so-called 'crisis' in education that has prompted so much attention in recent years may be explained by referring to the epistemological framework that underpins not only particular curricular and managerial developments but also the mechanisms for dealing with 'crisis' when it occurs. In other words, the mechanics of change may be located within the same epistemological framework that underpinned the particular policies and practices that led to the 'crisis'.

We may be left with a possibly relativistic determination of

educational ends in abstraction from a supposedly objectivistic determination of educational means. However, as I argue in the next
chapter, the so-called 'empirical' research procedure cannot enable us
to meet the criterion of objectivity assumed within the epistemic
framework of foundationalist empiricism and so I argue that we have
good reason to look for an alternative epistemology which coheres
with educational practices that are different from the ones criticized in
this chapter.

Notes and References

1 GELLNER, E. (1979) *Spectacles and Predicaments*, p. 39.
2 O'CONNOR, D.J. (1982) *Two Concepts of Education*, p. 144.
3 *Ibid.*, p. 139.
4 cf. HOLT, M. (1983) 'Vocationalism: The new threat to universal education'.
5 The Secretaries of State for Employment, Education and Science (Scotland and Wales) (1984) *Training For Jobs*, HMSO.
6 GLEESON, D. and MARDLE, G. (1980) *Further Education or Training?*, see
   especially ch. 1 and p. 116.
7 *Giving Youth A Better Chance*, 1979, Options for education, work and
   service: a report with recommendations of the Carnegie Council on
   policy studies in higher education.
8 This move was consolidated in: *A New Training Initiative: A consultative
   document*, MSC, 1981; *A New Training Initiative: An agenda for action*,
   MSC, 1981; *A New Training Initiative: A programme for action*, Cmnd
   8455, Department of Employment, HMSO, 1981. For a discussion of
   the implications of this initiative for FE, see the 'Introduction' to *Supporting YTS*, Further Education Unit (FEU), 1985, pp. 1–7. See also
   Vocational Preparation, FEU, 1981, especially p. 7 and section II.
9 GLEESON, D. and MARDLE, G., 1980, p. 124.
10 See CANTOR, L.M. and ROBERTS, I.F. (1979) *Further Education Today*
   RKP, ch. 1, for a review of such initiatives up to 1979. See *Publications*
   FEU, 1986, for a list of FEU titles which cover such initiatives in the
   1980s.
11 The Carnegie Council reported that 'there are substantial doubts that
   vocational education is generally effective, especially at the secondary
   level', 1979, p. 136.
12 *Ibid.*, p. 137.
13 OAKESHOTT, M. (1962) *Rationalism in Politics*, pp. 33–4.
14 FEU, 1981, p. 8.
15 Objective 3 of the *New Training Initiative* includes 'opening up widespread opportunities for adults, whether employed, unemployed or
   returning to work, to acquire, increase or update their skills and knowledge during the course of their working lives'. The DES 'Pickup'
   initiative may be seen to be related to this objective.

16 Increased emphasis is given to practical activity leading to the acquisition of skills. For example the FEU recommend that 'many of the young people will find the more general core objectives most accessible when approached through specific and practical activities', *A Basis for Choice*, FEU, 2nd edition, 1982, p. 21. Moreover these 'skills' are supposed to be transferable. 'A further major component of vocational preparation is the acquisition of basic skills.... These skills should be broad-based and transferable rather than specific and job-restricted', FEU, 1981, p. 13.

17 For example, as advocated by BACON, F. in the *Novum Organum* (many editions) and by DESCARTES, R. in *A Discourse on Method* (many editions).

18 cf. CORNBLETH, C. (1987) 'The persistence of myth in teacher education and teaching', in POPKEWITZ, T.S. (Ed.) *Critical Studies in Teacher Education* p. 193.

19 OECD (1985) *Education and Training after Basic Schooling*, p. 94.

20 cf. HAYES, C. *et al.* (1982) for the Institute of Manpower Studies *Foundation Training Issues. A Report for the MSC*. For a further discussion of this issue and for a useful list of selected references, see JOHNSTON, R. (1984) *Occupational Training Families: Their implications for FE*, FEU.

21 *Ibid.*, pp. 34–44.

22 *Ibid.*, pp. 42–3.

23 *Ibid.*, pp. 44–5.

24 For a more extensive critique of this issue, see JONATHAN, R.M. (1987) 'Core Skills in the Youth Training Scheme: An Educational Analysis'.

25 For a list of FEU publications write to:
Publications Despatch Centre
Department of Education and Science
Honeypot Lane
Canons Park
STANMORE
HA7 1AZ

26 JONATHAN, R.M., 1987.

27 GELLNER, E., 1979, p. 280.

28 *Ibid.*, p. 281.

29 *Ibid.*, p. 282.

30 *Ibid.*, p. 284.

31 See KATZNELSON, I. and WEIR, M. (1985) *Schooling for All*, ch. 8, for an account of the interrelationship between the educational and housing 'markets' in North America.

32 cf. ARNOWITZ, S. and GIROUX, H.A. (1986) *Education under Siege*; also APPLE, M.W. (1986) *Teachers and Texts*.

33 For example, the Open University, the Open Tech, some course submissions to the Council for National Academic Awards, Business and Technician Education Council (BTEC) and Scottish Vocational Education Council (SCOTVEC) curricula.

34 For a series of examples, see VINCENT, B. and VINCENT, T. (1985) *Information Technology and Further Education*.

35 The proximity of objectivism to mathematical positivism is readily apparent here. For example, 'Systems Theory' and 'Operational

Research' depend upon the notion that rational decision making is 'concerned with resolution of ambiguity and is synonymous with mathematical decidability' (WHITE, D.J., 1969, *Decision Theory*, p. 12). The idea that claims to know might be settled by appeal to a form of discourse within which disagreements are rare, is an idea that has much attraction for the objectivist. Mathematics seems to be just such a form of discourse. An objectivist might argue that the physical sciences are successful because claims about the way the world is can be settled by linking those claims with a mathematical equation whose solution is determinate. The objectivity of those claims is ensured because disputes rarely break out over the solution to an equation. The attractions of this argument are such that many economists operate within what Hahn and Hollis call 'orthodox Positivist tenets' (*Philosophy and Economic Theory*, 1979, p. 1).

Recently economists under the influence of G.L.S. SHACKLE (see especially his *Imagination and the Nature of Choice*, 1979, Edinburgh University Press), have begun to incorporate the effect of imagination within economic theory. Rather than attempting to quantify imagination and thus to work out a sophisticated algorithm for economic success, some economists have adopted the idea that economic success cannot be quantified. For example, EARL, P.E. (1984) *The Corporate Imagination*, Wheatsheaf, Brighton, presents an economic theory in the form of a series of case studies of successful economic practice and does not attempt to set out an algorithm linking economic theory and practice. For 'a revisionist's view of the economics of education', see MACE, J. (1984) *Higher Education Review*, Summer, pp. 39–56.

36   *Report into the Pay and Conditions of Service of School Teachers in Scotland,* chairman Sir Peter Main, presented to Parliament by the Secretary of State for Scotland, Oct. 1986, Cmnd. 9893. Edinburgh, HMSO, p. 9.
37   The issue of 'merit pay' for teachers is pertinent here, see also p. 106 in the *Report into the Pay and Conditions of Service of School Teachers in Scotland*, 1986, p. 106.
38   *Ibid.*, p. 35.
39   MACINTYRE, A. (1981) *After Virtue*.
40   *Ibid.*, p. 23.
41   At the time of writing, teacher shortages are reported in several parts of the UK and the number of teachers leaving the profession is at a record level (BBC TV News, 10 January 1990).

Chapter 3

Towards Interpretive Coherence

The previous two chapters have been concerned with the *present* state of educational theory and practice. Even though I have argued that much current educational theory and practice coheres with a foundationalist empiricist epistemology and its attendant research procedures, I have not developed the notion of coherence beyond an ordinary use of that word and its derivatives. In this chapter I begin to make up for that deficiency and to argue that educational theory may be 'scientific' without being 'objective'. The attraction of tying educational theory in with a procedure that is commonly assumed to produce our most useful and reliable theory — natural scientific theory — is clear enough. However, it is now widely accepted that empiricist accounts of theory production do not provide an adequate account of how natural scientists arrive at what is widely regarded as the most prestigious type of theory, let alone whether, and if so how, educational theorists might emulate that procedure.

I rehearse some theories of Popper, Lakatos, Feyerabend and Quine in order to argue that the utility and reliability of natural scientific theories cannot be underpinned by a reliance upon a foundationalist empiricist epistemology and its attendant research procedure. Instead of the empiricist idea that reliable theory is based on the secure foundations of supposedly theory-neutral observation statements, I argue that observation statements themselves are theoretically partisan and hence that theories are compared *against each other*. The philosophers mentioned above offer different solutions to the common problem of identifying those theories that form the standards against which others should be compared. I present their solutions in the form of a progressive argument that moves away from empiricist inductivism towards interpretive coherence.

I conclude that the holistic idea of maximizing the coherence of a 'network' of theory is of most interest to my developing account of educational theory. I offer a critique both of Quine's development of this idea and of the use that the Australian scholars Walker and Evers make of Quine's work in the development of a philosophy of education that they call 'materialist pragmatism'. While I argue against some of the conclusions that Walker and Evers draw, I suggest that their work opens up a fruitful line of enquiry into the nature and purpose of educational theory.

The Quinean idea of a network of theory which includes philosophical, scientific and ethical theories offers the possibility of moving away from the view that educational theorists might emulate the so-called 'empiricist' research procedure on the grounds that that procedure is responsible for the explanatory and predictive success commonly attributed to natural science — as if educational matters were static and simply waiting to be investigated, administered and evaluated in abstraction from the interests of educational practitioners. Instead, the possibility opens up of a range of educational theories in competition against one another, each offering different prescriptions for action in the dynamic contexts in which educational matters are practised.

Readers who are unfamiliar with the post-empiricist philosophy of science will find the sections on Quine and Materialist Pragmatism to be difficult. As these sections are crucial, I offer the following summary of their importance: Quine does not distinguish between theories and language. Nor does he recognize the idea of an external reality. For him, theories are compared against each other within a 'web' and the comparison is guided by the principle of maximizing overall coherence. The following analogy may be helpful: imagine that a pack of billiard balls represents your own particular 'web' of theories and that the cue ball represents a new theory or explanation — you accept the new theory or explanation into your 'web' if this acceptance means that you understand things better overall. Similarly, the cue ball is incorporated within the pack if its incorporation leads to a configuration of all the balls that was more compact than the original. For 'compact' read 'coherent' and the analogy is complete. If this explanatory analogy is unhelpful to you then a Quinean might conclude that the coherence of your 'web' was not increased by this explanation or 'theory'.

Quine is aware that his notion of coherence might appear vague and useless and so he attempts to make it operational and precise by suggesting a mathematical procedure whereby theories are formulated in a particular notation that is subject to certain logical rules.

However, I reject this suggestion and argue that it is preferable to envisage a web that comprises different forms of language and practices rather than to adopt what I see as another form of objectivism.

Empiricist Research

The central thesis behind empiricist research is that the world can be investigated by looking for regularities in its structure. These regularities may then be generalized into statements about what we know that are supposed to correspond with the way the world actually is. As a result we are supposed to be able to act and move in the world with increased efficacy. However, there are at least two major difficulties with this thesis. First, there is a difficulty with the notion that there can be a 'linking' of statements to the world, for we can never either in fact or in principle get beyond words to the world. Whatever we do we seem always to end up with a matching of statements to statements, since we have no access to the way the world actually is other than via the statements we use to describe the way that we actually perceive the world to be.

Second, the move postulated in empiricist inductivism from the particular to the general is logically inadequate as a guarantee of truth, because of the so-called problem of induction. No matter how many times something is seen to take place, that is no guarantee that that occurrence will always take place. Furthermore, since there are many occasions when the principle of induction has been deficient then, by itself, the principle of induction will always be deficient. Finally, in inductivism there is no case of induction where the principle of induction itself is not presupposed: it rests therefore on a blatant *petitio principii*.

In *The Logic of Scientific Discovery*[1] Popper claims he can overcome the problem of induction by pointing out that while no amount of careful observation of events can ever guarantee the truth of a statement that takes the form 'all Xs are Y', one observation of an X that is not a Y enables us to assert with logical security that 'not all Xs are Y'. This deceptively simple point reorients the scientific enterprise for Popper. Instead of scientists looking for confirming instances of a general statement or theory, Popper advocates that scientists start by making bold conjectures about an assumed generality and then set about trying to find a falsifying instance of that generality, so that they can be certain that they were wrong. Successive bold conjectures are made with the knowledge that some theories are false and so by a sort of negative implication conjectures asymptotically approach the truth though they never reach it.

Popper[2] likens truth to the summit of a mountain in that a climber or a truth-seeker may not know how near he is to the summit or indeed if he has even got there, yet his climbing implies that he recognizes that there is a summit. Now while the climber may not know whether he has reached the summit he can certainly check whether he has not yet reached it by attempts at falsification. Truth thus becomes in Popper's account of science a regulative principle towards which scientific progress evolves asymptotically. However, it is not just any truth to which Popper aspires; it is the search for 'interesting' truth that is important. For example:

> We are not content with 'twice two equals four', even though it is true ... what we are looking for are *answers to our problems*.[3] (original emphasis)

So for Popper content is also important; it is for this reason he introduces the notion of 'verisimilitude'[4] as the difference between the truth content of a theory and its falsity content. In other words, maximum 'verisimilitude' would only be obtained by a theory that was not only true but *comprehensively* true.[5]

The notion of 'verisimilitude', however, may be criticized on the grounds that it is 'theory-laden'. That is to say 'verisimilitude' seems to involve the recognition of a common framework within which to view not only matters of increased content but also to recognize falsifications when they occur. In terms of the mountain-climber analogy, we have to be sure that we are climbing the same mountain or at least mountains in the same group and that is something of which we cannot be sure since our framework only allows us to view our own mountain face and one mountain face may look much like another.

Popper accepts that

> at any moment we are prisoners caught in the framework of our theories ... but we are prisoners in a Pickwickian sense. If we try we can break out of our frameworks at any time[6]

and goes on to assert that, while the difficulty of discussion between people brought up in different frameworks is to be admitted, that difficulty does not make communication an impossibility; he does not think that much of scientific interest can be discovered by worrying what might be meant by 'in a Pickwickian sense'. It seems that for Popper, as long as we take care to state our theses as clearly as possible, we do not have to worry too much about language.[7] The idea that meaning might be relative to a framework is for Popper a bulwark of relativism.

The problem with this view is that many people do worry about language and for good reason. They see that the 'theory-dependence of observation statements' is really a problem about which part of a system of theories is to be modified and on what grounds, the solution to which is central to our coming to be able to give an account of scientific progress. The central difficulty with Popper's account of the logic of scientific discovery is that we have no access to a neutral observation language with which to test theory. Instead, observation is itself dependent upon the adoption of many auxiliary theories that serve to determine what might count as a valid observation. Popper is aware of this difficulty and attempts to solve it by suggesting that individual scientists or groups of scientists just accept certain observation statements as unproblematic 'background knowledge',[8] though Popper adds that this background knowledge can itself be challenged.[9]

However, this proposed solution does not really overcome the difficulty. Apart from the fact that an attempt to outline the logic of scientific discovery is somewhat weakened by a direct appeal to subjectivity of judgment, a new and highly innovative theory would never get started if it had to satisfy the same observational procedures that supported its predecessor. The idea that scientists would reject a well-established group of theories on the basis of one contradiction or what would be assumed to be one falsifying counter-instance is simply unbelievable, as Kuhn[10] has shown, not only because scientists do not happen to behave in that way but also because some of the best examples of scientific theory would on that basis have been rejected in their infancy. In effect, if Popper's account of falsification were accepted then scientific progress would seem to be impossible — experimental work would never 'get off the ground', so to speak.

Imre Lakatos attempted to account for a different preference in scientific theory by moving the emphasis from simple falsification of single theories towards the idea of the evolving changes and progression of groups of theories. Lakatos accepted that theories are compared with one another, not with an objective reality, but he attempted to account for the theory-dependence of observation statements by suggesting that scientists take a methodological decision to treat some theories as unproblematic while a new theory is under test.

This looks remarkably similar to Popper's proposed solution to the problem of the theory-dependence of observation statements. However, instead of treating theories in isolation, Lakatos suggested that we look at a 'research programme'[11] which consists, he says, of a series of theories that share the same 'hard core' of supposedly unproblematic content (axioms, basic postulates, central concepts, etc.), but which differ in their contributions to a 'protective belt' of content (auxiliary hypotheses, etc.) which needs to be altered progressively. As long as each modification of the protective belt enables us to predict new facts, some of which are corroborated by experiment, then the 'research programme' is considered to be 'progressing' and is supported by the scientific community. In this way, Lakatos claims he has elucidated the proper method for accounting for theory formation and progression and he suggests that this method is suitable for other types of theory as well as natural scientific theory.[12] In an educational context this suggestion has been taken up by Harris[13] and Matthews[14] who have attempted to use Lakatos's account of theoretic progression and change to prove the superiority of what they call a 'historical materialist research programme' in education. The extent to which these attempts are successful is contentious.[15]

However, as Feyerabend[16] has pointed out, just as theories can only be judged relative to other theories, so research programmes can only be judged relative to other research programmes. Unlike theory-comparison, time is needed in order to compare and evaluate research programmes. Lakatos admits that research programmes may degenerate for a while and then progress, so that time is needed before a research programme can be pronounced 'dead' or progressing. Indeed all research programmes would be 'still-born' unless time was allowed for their progression. The question arises as to how much time should be allowed? It seems it is only with the benefit of hindsight that Lakatos's methodology can be regarded as an adequate account for evaluating research programmes, in that at any instant it is not obvious whether a research programme is about to progress or continue to degenerate.

Lakatos's[17] immediate solution of withholding money and publication facilities as long as research programmes appear to be degenerating is hardly helpful, since money and publication facilities may be essential in order to determine whether or not a research programme is degenerating. Again one may question how long a research programme is to be 'nursed'.

For Feyerabend, the only method that allows the sort of progression in science which he believes Lakatos wants is the principle of 'anything goes'.[18] Feyerabend insists that Lakatos outlines 'the most advanced and sophisticated methodology in existence today'[19] but since even this methodology is held by Feyerabend to be inadequate, for the reasons advanced above, then he advocates the proliferation of theories so that there may be more opportunities for theory comparison. For Feyerabend, theoretical pluralism aids theoretical progression and it matters little whether mystics, magicians, theologians or scientists supply the theories that command our attention. Feyerabend argues that science is just

> one of the many forms of thought that have been developed by man, and not necessarily the best. It is conspicuous, noisy, and impudent, but it is inherently superior only for those who have already decided in favour of a certain ideology, or who have accepted it without having ever examined its advantages and its limits.[20]

The ideology to which Feyerabend refers includes the idea of universal reason based on science but this too is suspect.

> Given science, reason cannot be universal and unreason cannot be excluded. This feature of science calls for an anarchistic epistemology. The realization that science is not sacrosanct, and that the debate between science and myth has ceased without having been won by either side, further strengthens the case for anarchism.[21]

We might ask what Feyerabend might mean when he refers to a debate being won? If 'anything goes', and we have no reason to accept or reject anything finally other than our 'taste',[22] Feyerabend is left with an extreme form of relativism in which all theories, research programmes and ideologies (conceived as sorts of super-research programmes) are incommensurable. The difficulty for such extreme relativism is not simply that we seem to have nothing at our disposal with which to appraise any account of anything (including the claimed superiority of Feyerabend's methodology over Lakatos's methodology of scientific research programmes) but also that all accounts become incomprehensible unless there is at least some commensurability between them.[23] For example, we would not understand Feyerabend when he describes the Galileo–Bellarmine confrontation unless there were some commensurability between the ways in which Galileo, Bellarmine, Feyerabend and ourselves use the term 'faith'.[24] If Feyerabend is correct in arguing that previous scientific progress has

been achieved precisely because the accounts of Galileo and Bellarmine were incommensurable, then we should not be able to understand Feyerabend's thesis. As it is, however, Feyerabend's thesis is
comprehensible and must therefore be mistaken.

The Idea of Coherence within a Network of Theory

We have seen that the central problem that informs the work of these
post-empiricist philosophers of science concerns the theory-dependence of observation statements and the lack of an external 'touchstone' against which theories might be 'objectively' compared. We
have seen also that the solution that has been described as 'the most
advanced and sophisticated in existence today' fails to account for the
way in which scientific theories are compared against each other and
leads to the opposite suggestion that all theories are as valid as each
other. The above discussion has led us back to an impossible choice
between objectivism and relativism. I turn now to consider the work
of W.V.O. Quine for I believe that his work opens up a new line of
enquiry into the nature of scientific theory which may enable us to see
how to avoid confronting this impossible choice.

Rather than attempting to solve the problem of the theory dependence of observation statements, Quine attempts to dissolve this
problem by incorporating both theories and observation statements
within the same epistemological network. Using a metaphor that
closely resembles Wittgenstein's metaphor of 'fibres criss crossing',[25]
Quine suggests that knowledge forms a 'seamless web'[26] — a network
of belief, which forms a continuous whole, with theory which is less
amenable to revision by observation at the centre and observation
statements at the outside. The web continuously develops as new
pieces of evidence are incorporated into it. Claim and counter-claim
are part of the total body of theory and all theory is theory extension.

According to this account, children are born with some innate
dispositions, namely guidance by sensory stimuli, a taste for simplicity and a taste for conservation[27] that guide their learning of language.
Language learning is what Evers has called the 'entering wedge'[28] into
the process of scientific theory formation, and subsequent theory extension takes place by the accretion of the data occurring from sensory
stimuli. For Quine, 'we are working up our science from infancy
onward'.[29] However, there is an infinite number of ways that these
data can be incorporated within a developing network of theory —
sense data may cause perturbations across the network. (Using my

billiard ball analogy again, one might imagine a cue ball of observation striking a 'pack' of theory which is initially complicated before it rearranges itself into the simplest formation that most resembles the original configuration.)

Science is successful at modifying and extending our theory because it groups stimuli according to innately chosen similarities, which makes for successful inductions and fulfilled expectations. As Quine remarks:

> creatures inveterately wrong in their inductions have a pathetic but praiseworthy tendency to die before reproducing their kind.[30]

The importance of inductions for Quine is that they function as the entering point for the learning of language-and-theory and the anchor for subsequent development of language-and-theory. Learning thus takes place by the operation of a series of stimuli which are reinforced or extinguished according to whether they fulfil our expectations. According to this account ethical theories are equivalent to scientific theories. The 'ethical' problem of what to learn is considered to be logically equivalent to the 'scientific' problem of how to learn.[31] In both cases the guiding principle is the maximization of coherence of the developing network of theory.

We may question how theories that vary both in their semantics and in their ontological commitments may be situated within the same epistemological network. Quine's answer to this question comes in three parts: first, he argues against the notion of truth by virtue of meaning which he calls 'analyticity'.[32] Second, he argues that the coherence of our network of theories is maximized when our theories are translated into the canonical notation of first order predicate calculus.[33] Third, he argues in favour of something he calls the 'scientific method'.[34] I discuss each part in turn.

Quine's concerted attack on the notion of analyticity comes in his 'indeterminacy of radical translation thesis',[35] which involves him in the view that no reliable translations may exist between different languages. Quine argues that the reference of a general term in a remote language is objectively inscrutable because it depends on how one decides to translate a

> cluster of interrelated grammatical particles and constructions, plural endings, pronouns, numerals, the 'is' of identity and the adaptations 'since' and 'other'.[36]

To take an example, we have no reason for deciding that the utterance 'gavagai' in an alien native language refers to rabbits, undetached rabbit parts or rabbit stages or whatever. The only way Quine suggests we can determine which use is involved is by paying attention to the use of the word in sentences. This seems uncontroversial but Quine extends referential inscrutability into our own home language.

> We can systematically reconstrue our neighbour's apparent references to rabbits as really references to rabbit stages and his apparent references to formulas as really references to Gödel numbers and vice versa. We can reconcile all this with our neighbour's verbal behaviour by cunningly readjusting our translations of his various connecting predicates so as to compensate for the switch in ontology.[37]

Quine concludes that we can only question the reference of terms in a language by having recourse to some background language. But any attempt to justify our background language leads us to a regress which we can only stop by just accepting our mother tongue and taking its words at face value. However, if ordinary language forms the basis of our translations, then it seems as if we might have to accept ordinary language as telling us all that we need to know. But Quine's thesis[38] challenges this. As Romanos puts it:

> Our confident and effective utilization of our most familiar, all-inclusive ordinary language testifies . . . to the ultimate meaninglessness of . . . conceptual enquiry.[39]

Not only is there no one way the world really is but, for Quine, it no longer makes sense to say that there is a way we can really say it is.[40]

This argument against analyticity puts an end to the idea that something that we call 'meaning' is preserved when we translate between languages. For Quine, a scheme of translation is simply another theory that is tested according to whether it is the simplest way of reconciling the behaviour of those who speak in a different language with our own. This argument also puts an end to one of the central tenets of APE — that something is gained when the meaning of an educational term is analyzed. For Quine, such analysis can have no explanatory significance; just because we happen to be familiar with a particular way of speaking is no reason to suppose that that way has any epistemic privileges.

For these reasons and others, Quine dispenses with the notion of meaning and mentalistic semantics that rely on the notion of intention. Instead, Quine suggests that the coherence of our developing conceptual scheme is maximized when the ontological commitments of our theories are made explicit by translating all theories into the canonical notation of first order predicate calculus. Not only is this suggestion designed to show up contradictions within a theory, as happens for example when 'we find philosophers allowing themselves not only abstract terms but pretty unmistakable quantification over abstract objects ... and still blandly disavowing, within the paragraph, that there are such objects';[41] but also this suggestion is supposed to allow us to translate all theories into the same canonical notation.

Rather than the 'seamless web' being made up of theories that rely to varying degrees on intentional semantics and that are presented in a variety of notations, this suggestion allows Quine to have a 'seamless web' made up of theories that rely exclusively on extensional semantics and that are presented in the 'canonical notation', thus enabling him to give a determinate sense to the idea of maximizing coherence through the use of the term 'systematic virtue'. The literature that surrounds this term is vast and highly technical.[42] However, in summary, 'systematic virtue' is increased if the theory is simpler and does not involve logical contradiction. These two guiding principles are supposed to provide Quine with a way out of the regress of reasons inherent in foundationalist accounts of knowledge. It is the overall coherence of the theory to which we appeal rather than any purportedly epistemologically secure foundation.

It is important to notice that Quine does not suggest that the 'canonical notation' underpins our developing network of theory. Rather Quine suggests that we use the 'canonical notation' because it is a simplifying device with the same status as any other part of our network:

> the quest of a simplest, clearest overall pattern of canonical notation is not to be distinguished from a quest of ultimate categories, a limning of the most general traits of reality. Nor let it be retorted that such constructions are conventional affairs not dictated by reality; for may not the same be said of a physical theory? True, such is the nature of reality that one physical theory will get us around better than another, but similarly for canonical notations.[43]

For Quine, neither the meanings embodied in ordinary language, logical form nor theory-neutral observation statements serve as external touchstones with which to compare our network of theories. Now it looks as if Quine is suggesting that all modifications of our network of theories might be as good as each other. However, he attempts to avoid this relativistic conclusion through the notion of 'scientific method':

> Have we ... so far lowered our sights as to settle for a relativistic theory of truth ... brooking no higher criticism? Not so. The saving consideration is that we continue to take seriously our own particular aggregate science ... whatever it may be ... until by what is vaguely called scientific method we change ... for the better.[44]

Quine presents us with the idea that just as the infant's initial learning of language evolves into the adult's development of a network of theories, so this network also evolves from one generation to the next.

> Our patterns of thought ... have been evolving ... since the dawn of language; and ... we may confidently look forward to more of the same.[45]

In other words, Quine simply assumes that our science is evolving satisfactorily and relies upon what Gellner calls 'a pragmatic cheerfulness'[46] about the 'scientific method' guiding both the infant's learning of language and the conceptual inheritance of mankind. Presently, for Quine, the paradigm of 'scientific method' is provided by theoretical physics because theoretical physics is extensional and has been successful at satisfying his simplicity and conservation requirements.[47]

However, as Rorty notes, no one seriously expects that all true nomological statements can be derived from the laws of physics and so we have good reason to wonder why

> 'believes in ...' and 'translates as ...' owe more to the necessities of practice than 'is the same electron as ...' and 'is the same set as ...'? ... What is it that sets them apart, given that we no longer think of any sort of statement having a privileged epistemological status, but of all statements as working

together for the good of the race in that process of gradual holistic adjustment made famous by 'Two Dogmas of Empiricism'?[48]

The answer to this question may well be that Quine is interested in the idea that the world has a logical structure that may be mapped by a system of propositions formulated in the correct notation. For example, the fundamental particles of physics may be equivalent for Quine to the 'objects' that Wittgenstein describes in the *Tractatus Logico-Philosophicus*.[49] Despite his arguments to the contrary, Quine may well want 'logical form' to replace foundationalist empiricism as the supplier of a new 'grounding' for our theories.

Yet if Quine's holism were to lead him to the view that there are many different vocabularies available for describing 'reality' rather than the view that an extensional language is the exemplar for all others, then he would be able to find a role for philosophy as a supplier of those vocabularies. As it is philosophy, as we understand it, does not seem to have a role for Quine. However, aware of the paradox involved when a philosopher denies philosophy a role, Quine suggests that philosophers formulate theories about scientific theories — in other words philosophers make explicit in theory that which is implicit in (scientific) practice by making its theoretical commitments explicit and employing the canonical notation of extensional logic to do so.

Materialist Pragmatism

The central tenet of Materialist Pragmatism (MP) is an unreserved acceptance of Quinean pragmatism and epistemic holism, leading to the idea that educational theory develops as a response to the practical problems that arise in educational contexts. This idea is fused with a notion of egalitarianism in which there is a deliberate breaking down of professional hierarchies in order to facilitate access to problem-solving. Walker assumes that there is a variety of viewpoints/theories that compete to determine the orientation of educational policies and institutions and that these viewpoints, or theories as he prefers to call them,

> vary considerably in level of sophistication, scope of practice encompassed and applicability of content, as well as in degrees of commensurability or possibility for rational comparison and evaluation.[50]

Despite this variation Walker asserts that each theory will have something in common with other theories. This area of overlap he terms, following Lakatos, 'touchstone'.[51] Walker uses this term in order to stress that two theories may only be compared when their proponents can recognize common standards such as common theoretical claims and methodologies and findings produced by the application of such methodologies — 'evidence'. According to Walker, at present we do not have — but most urgently need — some 'touchstone' for educational problems and their solution. In other words, we urgently need some agreed methodological criteria for settling what is and what is not to count as overlap between competing criteria and theories. Walker suggests 'logic, semantics and epistemology'[52] as starting points for getting the procedure of theory-comparison going. When we have some 'touchstone' we can set about the task of proposing theories along with the task of agreeing the further 'touchstone' that might be used to settle disputes between competing alternative educational theories.

The coherence of an overall conceptual scheme is the guiding principle for such a Quinean programme for philosophy of education. By this canon such a programme is supposed to cohere better than APE in the sense that our developing network of theory is simpler and our educational problems are more easily solved if MP is substituted for APE. In the same way as the positing of molecules simplifies the description of material objects, molecules are incorporated into the scheme having the same status as ethical judgments and systems of canonical notation and anything else that helps us to 'get us around better'.[53] The much discussed problem of educational theories involving means and ends and the supposed distinction between science and ethics is dissolved in Quine's semantic web since both are amenable to scientific investigation.

There are, however, problems with MP which Evers acknowledges. For example, your conceptual scheme and mine may not be identical since we have been subject to different stimuli. How are our differences to be reconciled? According to Evers, we firstly maximize the 'systematic virtue' of our schemes by being persuaded of the value of putting everything into canonical notation. This may reveal logical inconsistencies. If it does not then we reduce our values into methods and substance amenable to scientific investigation. While Quine is pessimistic that there will always be some residual value-conflict unresolved, Evers suggests that we can always ask: Does this ultimately valued state of affairs aid in the solution of problems?[54]

Since good science requires that we value problem-solving, we give priority to problem-solving in educational theorizing. This apparently can be used to settle the value-conflict but someone may protest, for example, that our best scientific theory may change what we ordinarily mean by good and bad. This is highly desirable for Evers, because at least our best theory may have 'winnowed the chaff of superstition and nonsense'.[55] Indeed, for Evers, what we ordinarily mean by good and bad is their role in our best theory. Ordinary use is use within a theory. For example, language and theory are equivalent for Evers and so one or the other can drop out of use. Just as intentions are equivalent to physical states, so one or the other can drop out of use unless it serves as a sort of useful shorthand.

There is also the objection that Evers' position may be regarded as relativist. Evers accepts that in the end we just 'fight it out'.[56] We cannot claim

> any higher truth than the truth that we are claiming or aspiring
> to as we continue to tinker from our system of the world
> within. If ours were one of two rival best theories, it would be
> our place to insist on the truth of ours and the falsity of the
> other theory where it conflicts.[57]

This may not seem to be a relativist position. We might remember, however, that the notion of meaning is empty for Evers and that when a final statement of disagreement is reached there are no means of gaining further insight into the subject of the disagreement, in as much as appeals to science and behavioural evidence have been exhausted.

This seems to be a debilitating criticism of MP, for the notion of meaning at least allows us to account for understanding with disagreement. The idea of 'touchstone' theory mentioned earlier is only helpful if we can recognize and apply 'touchstone' to other parts of our conceptual scheme in order to solve our problems. If we recognize and apply 'touchstone' by even more 'touchstone' then we seem again to be involved in a regress similar to that that takes place in foundationalism. MP may be based on the idea of coherence but crucial to it seems to be the parallel foundation of mutual commitment to finding and consistently holding to 'touchstone' theory while a problem is solved and the sands of overall theory have shifted. It is true that we can only tinker with our world from within but, in order to make progress with that tinkering, we must elevate some theory, whether it be the touchstone theory of rationality, logical form or whatever above all others, at least until a problem is solved.

This elevation may appear to be a very modest tilt in the direction of foundationalism since, within MP, the 'foundations' may be replaced in the same way that any part of a conceptual scheme may be replaced. However, without some idea of what would count as a solution to a problem it is hard to see how commitment to a particular touchstone theory is to be sustained. At what point are we to abandon one account of 'touchstone' in favour of another? Furthermore, how are problems to be recognized, selected and tackled? Within MP, any problem that is extensional is a practical problem but if material constraints are sufficient to decide the order of problem-solving then it seems hard for MP to avoid the conclusion that material constraints function as at least one sort of foundation upon which edifices of conceptual coherence may be built.

I detect a difference in the approaches of Walker and Evers to this issue. For example, Walker suggests

> that serious consideration be given to a totally (social) relationist theory of the individual, in which skills, habits, traits and other personal characteristics are stated purely as social relations.[58]

In this Walker seems to be more of a pragmatist than Evers and to avoid the reductionist epistemology of Quine who proposes that

> causal explanations of psychology are to be sought in physiology, of physiology in biology, of biology in chemistry, and of chemistry in physics — in the elementary physical states.[59]

In contrast, Evers considers that the notion of intention may in time be identified materialistically as a series of physical causes[60] and so it might if Quine's programme of conceptual revision were to be carried out *prior* to any empirical investigation — thus eliminating the dualist metaphysics inherent in ordinary language by regimenting it into the canonical notation. However, as Malcolm notes:

> the admission ... that some revision of language is required in order to establish the identity conjecture as true is an admission that it is not a logical possibility that the conjecture should be established as contingently true or as contingently false.[61]

The point is that the move to a canonical notation is presupposed in Evers' consideration and far from this being the kind of neutral simplifying device that Evers, Walker and Quine seem to suppose it to be, in fact their use of it has already decided in favour of particular sorts of investigation. However, there appears to be no more logical reason to adopt the conceptual revision of ordinary language into canonical notation than there is to adopt the conceptual revision within ordinary language that can lead to statements like 'tables lay eggs or [that] eggs lay tables'.[62]

My criticism of MP has been directed against the Quinean idea of a network of theory that is supposed to develop in an evolutionary way as 'problems' are solved by applying something called the 'scientific method' that turns out to have reached its best formulation in theoretical physics. Quine's work, however, opens new lines of enquiry into the nature of educational theory. It may be possible to extend Quine's metaphor of a 'seamless web' to the elucidation of the logic of educational theory without imagining that the fibres of the web are all of the same kind, namely strands in a logical calculus. Furthermore, such a possibility might allow us to account for the way in which parts of the 'web' can function as 'assumptions' on which other parts of the 'web' are based — as key threads in the overall fabric.

In other words, the metaphor of a theoretic 'network' might be accepted whilst MP's claim to have found the method of theoretical comparison in an educational context might be abandoned. A remark of Sellars[63] might be paraphrased to point the way forward: educational theorizing is rational not because it has a foundation of a fixed methodology or a fixed commitment to the inscrutability of certain types of theoretical predicates but because it is a self-correcting enterprise that can put any claim in jeopardy though not all claims at the same time and not always in the same way. What is needed is an account of the way in which terms from a variety of discourses can come to function as inter-discursive touchstones of rationality.

It might now be helpful to discuss how the conclusions reached in this chapter have a bearing on my developing account of educational theory and practice. In the previous chapter I argued that consumerism, vocationalism, managerialism and objectivism cohere in the sense that they are consistent with each other and internally connected. However, the trenchant criticism that can be directed against this set of theories and practices may be taken as an indication of a lack of coherence between this set and accepted methods of argument. The notion of maximizing coherence has been developed as a characteristic of the development of natural scientific theory and I have begun to show how this development might be emulated by educational theorists.

We have moved away from foundationalist empiricism on the grounds that natural science is not underpinned by foundationalist empiricist epistemology and that the empiricist account of theory-production does not properly characterize the activity of natural scientists. We have seen also how the 'objectivism' implied in Lakatos's 'methodology of scientific research programmes' leads Feyerabend to out and out relativism. Instead, we have considered some aspects of Quine's philosophy and the use that Walker and Evers make of it within 'materialist pragmatism' on the grounds that this approach overcomes the 'theory-ladenness' problem and presents a synthesis of different types of theory within the same network, thus offering the possibility of a non-foundationalist and non-objectivist account of theory-comparison.

I argued that there is a tension within Quine's work between the idea that 'logical form' functions as a kind of 'foundation' for the edifice of theoretic coherence and the idea that there are no theory-neutral devices that can serve as foundations for theory-extension within a theoretic network. I went on to argue that this tension is brought into prominence when consideration is given to the particular form of pragmatism adopted by the proponents of Materialist Pragmatism which suggests that our theories develop as a response to the problems that we face.

As I pointed out, problems are framed according to the theories that are likely to be relevant to their solution. However, the adoption of Quine's conservation and simplicity requirements leads to the view that it is impossible to frame a problem that questions the very criteria for what might count as a solution. Yet it can be argued that it is precisely this kind of problem that yields the most fruitful theoretic advances. For example, periods of what Kuhn calls 'revolutionary science'[64] characterize periods of 'crisis' within the scientific community in which a number of theoretical frameworks or 'paradigms' compete to determine what might count as a problem.[65] To take another example, the Enlightenment is seen by Gellner[66] to embody a radical break with tradition, that leads to a clear distinction between developed and underdeveloped societies — with clear advantages for the former. In contrast, Quine seems to place too much emphasis on the idea that continuous scientific evolution can be assumed. His conservation and simplicity requirements seem to be biased in favour of the solution of problems whose form is immediately apparent, for these requirements seem to militate against any theoretical extravagance however useful such extravagance might turn out to be in the long term.

In the next chapter I intend to substantiate the claim that educational, natural scientific and other types of theory form a network that is neither bound using the 'canonical notation' nor bound according to the posits of theoretical physics. Instead, I argue in favour of an account of natural science due to T.S. Kuhn who explains discontinuity in theory extension by invoking the notions of interpretation and shared commitment within the natural scientific community. Rather than the boundaries of natural science being sharply drawn, I argue that the interpretation of scientific terms depends upon a 'family resemblance' between natural scientific and other linguistic practices. I conclude that there are good reasons to adopt the metaphor of a theoretic network which includes all types of theory and to adopt a Kuhnian account of natural science as a model for theorizing about education.

Notes and References

1   POPPER, K.R. (1968) *The Logic of Scientific Discovery*.
2   TARSKI, A. (1944) 'The semantic conception of truth'.
3   POPPER, K.R. (1963) *Conjectures and Refutations*, pp. 229–30.
4   *Ibid.*, p. 219.
5   While pragmatic considerations may guide the kind of conjectures that scientists make, for Popper the truth of those conjectures is unrelated to such 'subjective' considerations. Instead, Popper subscribes to Tarski's (1944) semantic theory of truth. Popper has a particular interpretation of Tarski that is not shared by other philosophers. For one overview see HAACK, S. (1978) *Philosophy of Logics*, Cambridge University Press, especially pp. 112–22. See also STRAWSON, P.F. (1970) *Meaning and Truth*; and DAVIDSON, D. (1984) 'True to the facts', in *Inquiries into Truth and Interpretation*, pp. 37–54.
6   POPPER, K.R. (1970) 'Normal science and its dangers', in LAKATOS, I. and MUSGRAVE, A. (Eds) *Criticism and the Growth of Knowledge*, p. 56.
7   Popper thinks that essentialist theories of meaning have little explanatory value. See 'A long digression concerning essentialism' in his autobiography *Unended Quest*, 1976, pp. 18–31.
8   POPPER, K.R., 1963, p. 238.
9   *Ibid.*
10 KUHN, T.S. (1962) *The Structure of Scientific Revolutions*, especially ch. 2.
11 LAKATOS, I. (1978) *The Methodology of Scientific Research Programmes*.
12 *Ibid.*, especially ch. 2.
13 HARRIS, K. (1979) *Education and Knowledge*.

14 MATTHEWS, M.R. (1980) *The Marxist Theory of Schooling*.
15 cf. Reviews by BARROW, R. (1981) *Journal of Curriculum Studies*, 13, 4, p. 371; and ASPIN, D.N. (1980) *Comparative Education* 16, 2, pp. 171–8.
16 FEYERABEND, P.K. (1978) *Science in a Free Society*.
17 LAKATOS, I., 1978, p. 117.
18 FEYERABEND, P.K. (1975) *Against Method*, p. 10.
19 *Ibid.*, p. 145.
20 *Ibid.*, p. 15.
21 *Ibid.*, p. 14.
22 *Ibid.*, p. 285.
23 Note that this criticism may also be directed at Popper's account.
24 FEYERABEND, P.K., 1975, discusses this at length, see especially pp. 192–3, where he refers to 'Galileo's headlong precipitancy in forcing an issue that might trouble the faith of the simple'. Here as elsewhere Feyerabend assumes that we understand the role that the term 'faith' played in the lives of Galileo and Bellarmine.
25 WITTGENSTEIN, L. (1953) *Philosophical Investigations*, p. 32.
26 QUINE, W.V.O. (1951) 'Two dogmas of empiricism' reprinted in *From a Logical Point of View*, 1953, and henceforth cited as in that volume. In this instance see p. 42.
27 QUINE, W.V.O. (1974) *The Roots of Reference*, p. 137. See also QUINE, W.V.O. (1960) *Word and Object*, p. 23.
28 EVERS, C.W. (1984) 'Epistemology and justification: From classical foundationalism to Quinean coherentism and materialist pragmatism', in EVERS, C.W. and WALKER, J., p. 22.
29 QUINE, W.V.O., 1974, p. 138.
30 QUINE, W.V.O. (1969) *Ontological Relativity and Other Essays*, p. 126.
31 EVERS, C.W. (1982) *Logical Structure and Justification in Educational Theory*, ch. 6 contains a fuller discussion of this issue.
32 This is one of the 'dogmas of empiricism' that Quine attacks in QUINE, W.V.O., 1953, pp. 20–46. The other dogma is 'reductionism'.
33 cf. QUINE, W.V.O., 1960, pp. 228–41.
34 *Ibid.*, pp. 23–5.
35 See QUINE, W.V.O., 1960, ch. 2; and QUINE, W.V.O., 1969, ch. 1.
36 QUINE, W.V.O., 1969, p. 32.
37 *Ibid.*, p. 47.
38 Especially his 'Ontological Relativity' thesis in QUINE, W.V.O., 1969.
39 ROMANOS, G.D. (1983) *Quine and Analytic Philosophy*, p. 96.
40 Quine would therefore be unimpressed by G.E. MOORE's (1959) argument in 'Proof of an External World' in his *Philosophical Papers*. For Quine, Moore touches neither the issue of absolute ontology nor absolute semantics.
41 QUINE, W.V.O., 1960, p. 241.
42 For a discussion of the use that Quine makes of this term see EVERS, C.W., 1984, especially p. 3 and the footnotes on that page.
43 QUINE, W.V.O., 1960, p. 161.
44 *Ibid.*, pp. 24–5.
45 QUINE, W.V.O., 1969, p. 24.
46 GELLNER, E. (1979) *Spectacles and Predicaments*, pp. 241–62.

47 See Quine's argument in his 'Facts of the Matter', 1977.
48 RORTY, R. (1980) *Philosophy and the Mirror of Nature*, p. 201.
49 WITTGENSTEIN, L. (1961) *Tractatus Logico-Philosophicus*.
50 WALKER, J.C. (1984) 'Dusting Off Educational Studies: A methodology for implementing certain proposals of John Wilson's', p. 5.
51 This notion, which originates in the work of Lakatos, is central to MP and features in most MP publications, see for example p. 5 of above. For a list of MP publications see bibliography under EVERS, C.W. and WALKER, J.C., 1984.
52 WALKER, J.C., 1984, p. 12.
53 QUINE, W.V.O., 1960, p. 250.
54 EVERS, C.W., 1982, pp. 314–8.
55 *Ibid.*
56 *Ibid.*
57 *Ibid.*
58 WALKER, J.C. (1984) 'The development and exercise of personal autonomy: An extensional equivalence' in EVERS, C.W. and WALKER, J. p. 136.
59 QUINE, W.V.O., 1977, p. 169.
60 EVERS, C.W. (1984) 'Naturalised epistemology and neural principles of learning: Towards a congruence', in EVERS, C.W. and WALKER, J., pp. 137–42.
61 MALCOLM, N. (1972) *Problems of Mind*, p. 72.
62 *Ibid.*
63 SELLARS, W. (1963) *Science Perception and Reality*, p. 170.
64 KUHN, T.S., 1962.
65 Of interest here is the debate between Kuhn and Popper, the subject of which concerns the status of scientists as solvers of 'problems' or 'puzzles'. This debate is recorded in LAKATOS, I. and MUSGRAVE, A. (Eds) 1970.
66 GELLNER, E. (1974) *Legitimation of Belief*.

Chapter 4

Rationality

In the previous chapter I argued that foundationalist empiricism should be rejected in favour of holistic coherence as an epistemological underpinning of natural science. In the course of that argument I was able further to explicate the notion of coherence as that notion might be applied to linguistic practice generally. In this chapter I argue that rationality is closely connected to the overall coherence of our thoughts and activities that include words and actions, theories and practices.

Already we have rejected two forms of objectivism which suggest that the notion of coherence can be made precise. At the beginning of this chapter I pursue, without success, the idea that objectivism might be possible if criteria could be set out in advance of the problem to which they are to be applied so that they may serve as 'foundations' for rational behaviour. Having rejected what I see as the only plausible accounts of objectivism, I go on to examine the nature of practical knowledge and to explain how that sort of knowledge leads some theorists to fear the spectre of relativism. Then I move beyond objectivism and relativism[1] by discussing T.S. Kuhn's interpretive account of natural science. This discussion enables me to hold on to the idea that some societies and some practices are more rational than others without implying that any particular network of theories and practices will be always more coherent and hence more rational than alternatives.

In some ways this extended discussion of the notion of rationality fits uneasily with my developing account of educational theory and practice for I am trying to get away from the 'theory guiding practice' idea which suggests that a long and detailed explication of one notion can help clear up many difficulties with the application of other notions that might be relevant to us in the future. However, I believe that objectivistic presuppositions are so firmly woven into our 'web' of theories and practices that it is necessary carefully to try to 'unpick' these presuppositions before they may finally be removed. Moreover the notion of 'rational' may serve as a useful shorthand way of describing what seems to matter most — that we can tell some true stories and that we can choose in morally propitious ways.

The importance of these arguments might be illustrated by a discussion of the ways in which some educational decisions are made: it might be imagined that teachers are the only people qualified to make such decisions since it is only they who are 'on the inside' of educational forms of discourse.[2] This way presupposes the pragmatic idea that problems may only be solved in the particular contexts in which those problems arise and the relativistic idea that the solutions offered vary according to the particular membership of the group of teachers concerned. Plainly this view would be unacceptable to those parents whose children were affected by the proposed solutions. Those parents might, with some justification, come to consider that their children's future was being determined according to the 'prejudices' of a group of teachers.[3] Alternatively it might be imagined that teachers should be obliged to specify and work to a list of criteria that are made available to all interested parties. An objectivist might support this way of prescribing teaching practice and appraising performance within it.

It is not difficult to see that the topics of rationality and theory-preference are fused in the idea that rational action is secured on the basis of the best account of the way the world actually is, as opposed to acting in accordance with our private impulses or anybody else's desires. It is this idea that lies behind objectivism and leads us to be suspicious of the alternative idea which suggests that theories are to be preferred on the basis of criteria that are internal to an investigative community. I argue that we need to give up the way of looking at theory appraisal that leads us towards an impossible choice between either criteria that are supposed to exist apart from any community or a community that is supposed to encompass internal or 'tacit' criteria that do not impinge in any way upon other communities. I conclude the chapter by arguing that there are no substantive differences between theoretical and practical interest and that there are no necessary distinctions between the interpretation of social or natural phenomena.

Why Objectivism is Impossible

We have already seen that the notions of 'experience' and 'logical form' cannot enable us to achieve a position of permanent 'cosmic exile'[4] from which to view a developing network of theory 'objectively'. Here I argue against another attempt to outline a form of objectivism through the idea that criteria for rationality are universally applicable. This argument is meant to be conclusive against any form of objectivism.

Let us first examine some of the specific claims that have been made concerning the existence of criteria of rationality.[5]

Consistency

Winch[6] considers the possibility of the independent existence of what he calls 'inter-forms of life' touchstones or criteria of rationality, such as the criterion that rationality should involve consistency. This criterion can be dismissed by pointing out that the recognition of consistency depends upon a shared theoretical background that enables us to recognize an inconsistency: for example, to recognize that there is an inconsistency in my unlocking the front door whilst saying that I am switching on the light depends upon a shared background of assumptions regarding switches, wiring, locks, doors and so on. A further reason to reject this criterion is that rationality is not a concept that can be applied to individual acts. We are tolerant of individual inconsistencies: others may sometimes be inconsistent, but we do not always dismiss them as irrational. Even if someone were to be consistent in being inconsistent, we should be unable to know how to apply a criterion of consistency without some further appraisal of their behaviour.

Logical Contradiction

While logical contradictions may be recognized within one form of discourse (the paradigm being in Boolean algebra), the need to translate other forms of discourse into a form where contradictions might be recognized always leaves open the possibility that the translation scheme introduces its own logical inconsistencies. This conclusion also follows from Quine's 'indeterminacy of radical translation' thesis.[7] However, as Putnam has pointed out,[8] Quine's thesis would only be plausible in the hypothetical case of an alien culture with no interests common to our own. As it is, however, Quine's thesis is implausible because human beings do share common interests. As I shall argue, while it may not be possible to provide universal 'logical' criteria for rationality, common interests between translator and translated are sufficient to make translation more determinate than Quine suggests is possible and to make some 'logical' criteria for rationality appropriate in particular contexts.

Falsehood

The recognition of a falsehood seems to be similarly context-dependent. For example, in a scientific context a statement asserting the truth of the doctrine of transubstantiation is false: in a religious context a statement about transubstantiation may be held to be true. Now both rationalists and empiricists have traditionally searched for the one form of enquiry that acts as a 'final court of appeal' for all others and is able to settle matters such as this; for without a 'final court of appeal' truth seems to be equivalent to contextually specific consensus. I shall argue that this is indeed the case but that there are good reasons for preferring certain contexts over others for the purpose of evaluating claims to truth. In this I shall hold Habermas's[9] consensus theory of truth to be important.

Nonsense

Ascertaining the sense of a statement seems to be prior to and hence irrelevant to the determination of its rationality. Claims to rationality may only be decided for statements that make some sense. That is not to say that there has to be no doubt about the sense of an expression before its claim to rationality can be decided. There will always be the possibility of doubt. Rather it is to say that those who judge claims to rationality must have a prior idea of the sense of the statement(s) concerned.

Coherence

The problem with this criterion is that it may only be applied intra-theoretically. Any attempt to establish this criterion as an inter-theoretical criterion generates a regress. This is because all statements and actions appear free-floating and apparently random until they are viewed from some particular theoretical perspective. There is thus a need for a further theory to allow coherence to get a purchase as an inter-theoretical criterion. This further theory, however, itself requires a further theory in order to establish its own coherence and so on. My earlier discussion of Quine's work is relevant here: I argued that the notion of coherence cannot function as an inter-theoretical criterion of rationality without a position of at least temporary 'cosmic exile' being assumed by the theorist.

Teleology

The adjectives 'rational' and 'irrational' only apply to people and things that people intend to do.[10] Hence we can say that curricular developments are rational but not accidents. Now as it is always possible to ascribe intentionality retrospectively to what we see as rational and irrational people, thoughts, words and deeds, then 'teleology' becomes a criterion in all cases and therefore ceases to have any particular explanatory power as a criterion for rationality generally, except at the very lowest level as a characteristic feature of all human actions.

Adequacy of Reason

This criterion seems to start an infinite regress of criteria. In order to apply it there is a need for a criterion for adequacy that in turn may only be applied according to a further criterion for adequacy and so on into a regress that is halted when someone simply acts. For example, within educational institutions there is a variety of viewpoints that compete to determine what shall be done in the name of education, not just those of individual teachers who might not be expected to justify every decision that they make as part of their professional practice, but also those of parents, political parties, religious denominational groups and so on who might express views, the contentiousness of which places educational policy-makers in the position of having to provide justificatory arguments to support their decisions. It seems to me that there are five such types of argument that might be mounted in such a case. I outline these below along with a brief *critique* of their adequacy when considered in isolation from one another and from the context in which a particular decision is to be justified.

1　We appeal to the personal authority of someone with a record of sound judgment and experience. The problem with this step is that we need some means of agreeing on our recognition of such a person and on the limits we wish to set to their authority.

2　We appeal to the authority of some group of individuals with similar record and experience. Again we have a difficulty in agreeing on our recognition of such individuals and recognizing when their claim to authority should be limited or overturned, particularly when that involves our querying and rejecting of our own right to pronounce as in the case of an appeal to a group of which we are members.

3　We appeal to the desirable consequences that we believe might follow from the adoption of a particular course of action. The problem here is that we do not seem to be successful at prediction in the social sphere. That is why Popper[11] advocates 'piecemeal approaches' to social planning with constant reassessments of courses of action.[12] The problem with Popper's suggestion is that we do not know how often such reassessments should be made. As Lakatos[13] points out, time is needed before a development can be regarded as having come to fruition.

4　We appeal to a concern that all groups interested in a particular problem might be thought or said to share and attempt to show how one course of action is more in accord with that concern than others. This is roughly the procedure advocated by the proponents of MP that was discussed and criticized in the previous chapter.

5　We assemble all possible accounts of data and phenomena bearing on our decision, lay out all the relevant features and attempt to assign weightings to each in the hope that mathematical decidability can be invoked as a means of ensuring objectivity of judgment. However, this step involves a criterion of completeness that cannot be satisfactorily applied. For example, it is doubtful whether we can ever know that we have assembled all the relevant alternatives and what basis can be given for weighting other than that of interests, which may already be said to presuppose a preference for one particular course of action.

From the above discussion we may conclude that even though these criteria of rationality may be applicable in specific contexts, their application always introduces a contingency that negates their claim to universality. Let us now examine whether this contingency can be eliminated by setting out rules of procedure that govern their own application as well as the application of criteria: Wittgenstein's use of the term 'language-game' draws our attention to the importance of the interweaving of actions and words within language. If it were the case that rules exist prior to anyone's engaging in a language-game and serve to define every move in the subsequent game, then it is difficult to see how children could ever begin to learn their native language or how anyone could speak in an unfamiliar situation without learning such a set of 'anterior' rules first. (But how could they do that without already having learned language? — a *reductio ad adsurdum*.)

While there are formal rules like grammatical rules and the (written) rules of a game, these by no means govern the game or define its limits. For example, people can still be playing tennis after considerable modification of the rules and this modification can take place while they are playing. As Rizvi points out:

> while learning a game may entail explicitly learning its rules, it *need not*; one might learn them by observation and practice. But crucially rules cannot be learnt or made explicit in an abstraction, in a context-free situation.[15] (original emphasis)

This context-dependence suggests a paradox, to which Wittgenstein refers:

> This was our paradox! No course of action could be determined by a rule, because every course of action can be made out to accord with the rule.[16]

Kripke[17] interprets Wittgenstein's 'private language argument'[18] in a way that is helpful in our attempts to understand this paradox in Wittgenstein's idea of following a rule. He draws attention to the fact that our grasping of a rule comes from a definite number of cases yet the rule we grasp and the way we understand it is going to govern its application in an infinite number of cases in the future. For example, how do I know that when I recognize a tower that that recognition is in accord with my past recognition of towers? To this sceptical problem, Wittgenstein suggests a sceptical solution. The assertion 'Jones means tower by "tower"' cannot mean anything for an individual. Our naive intuition that we know what we mean is undermined by the sceptical solution. It follows that, in order to follow a rule, it must be possible to check whether a rule is being followed and that presupposes a communal form of discourse within which rules evolve as the form of discourse develops. Hence, it is not possible to set out rules once and for all that remain ossified within a 'statute book' divorced from the practical forms of discourse in which they are supposed to be applied.

This impossibility is debilitating to all forms of objectivism, whether these depend upon the existence of one permanent neutral framework of enquiry, form of discourse or set of criteria to which we can ultimately appeal in order to determine the nature of rationality. In each case, their application in context is interwoven with, and as important as, their formulation. Any attempt to 'objectify' that application always generates a logically regressive chain of frameworks, forms of discourse or sets of criteria, all purporting to 'objectify' the application of their predecessors in the chain.

Practical Knowledge and Relativism

We have seen how the empiricist idea that theory should guide educational practice has led to the assumption that theory is somehow prior to practice and that if only we could get the theory of education 'right', appropriate, efficient and suitable, practice would follow. However, recent difficulties encountered in attempts to give an account of educational theory have prompted some philosophers of education to look at the question of the nature and scope of practice.[19]

Hirst,[20] for example, believes that educational practice can be improved if 'practical' or 'tacit' kinds of knowledge are made explicit.[21] By giving an account of the 'logic' of practical discourse through empirical research of 'operationally effective'[22] current practice, Hirst supposes that 'rationally defensible principles'[23] will be elicited or emerge, against which future practice may be judged. It is not difficult to see the attractions that this kind of delineation of rational practice has for Hirst and others. If it is accepted that practical knowledge is an unformalizable, yet essential part of any practice, then it looks as if there can never be any objective way of evaluating practices against one another unless practical knowledge can be made explicit and hence amenable to rational argument.

For example, current educational practice is much influenced by the idea that objectivity is ensured by the constant application of a set of criteria or algorithms; hence there is a proliferation of policy statements all purporting to supply a 'statute book' of criteria. The trend towards criterion-referenced assessment may be seen as a special case of this proliferation: it is widely assumed that the performance of a task can be matched with a statement of competence, and believed that such a procedure is more 'objective' than the procedure whereby an accomplished practitioner observes an apprentice and offers to report on his progress.

The reservation that such assessment criteria might be subject to some indeterminacy of interpretation seems not to deter some of the proponents of criterion-referenced assessment. These proponents do not seem to question whether, and if so how, the availability of a list of performance criteria[24] necessarily secures or promotes the 'objectivity' of the assessment. In their view objectivity is ensured by the matching of actions with impersonal criteria, both of which may be supposed to exist apart from the conventions and norms operating in any community of practitioners who might be thought to have an interest in the assessment and thus to be the ones to determine what counts as 'objective' within it.

These recent moves towards this form of objectivism in educational practice may be a reflection of a deep distrust of the notion of practical judgment. Objectivists may be deluded in thinking that practical knowledge can be formalized in order to make educational practices precise and their delusion may lead them to formalize procedures which, when operationalized, have the effect of suggesting that debate about the best course of action in a practical context is otiose unless it is concerned with the application of a set of technical rules. However, as we have seen, the outcome of such a debate cannot be to determine the best course of action objectively. Instead, the net effect of unduly restricting practical discourse in this way may be to lead practitioners to a sense of hopelessness that their practices are, after all, relative to the particular set of rules to which they are supposed to work and in whose formulation they have played little part.

In the next chapter I attempt to substantiate this hypothesis. I turn now to consider T.S. Kuhn's account of natural science for I believe that his account offers the starting-point for providing an account of natural science as a practice that moves us beyond objectivism and relativism. I go on to argue that there are sufficient similarities between practices for all practitioners to share a general sense of 'community' that could enable them rationally to establish their priorities if the grip that the notions of objectivism and relativism have on their thinking were to be slackened.

T.S. Kuhn's Account of Natural Science

Kuhn has produced two major publications, *The Structure of Scientific Revolutions*[25] and later *The Essential Tension*,[26] in which he supplements and modifies his earlier work. The early Kuhn is often considered to be advocating a similar thesis to that of Feyerabend, in that both writers refer to incommensurability and pluralism and are consequently often accused of advocating relativism. In Kuhn's case this accusation arises because of his insistence that it is only the scientific community which is in a position to decide which theories and normal working practices are to be adopted. In other words, Kuhn adopts an 'elitist' solution to the problem of appraising and evaluating scientific theories.

The notion of a 'paradigm' is central to Kuhn's work. However, for Kuhn the term 'paradigm' takes on a number of different meanings,[27] of which three are central. Paradigm (sense 1) refers to those theories that the scientific community take to be unproblematic and against which other theories are tested. Paradigm (sense 2) refers to those practices which the scientific community takes to be unproblematic, for example basic measurement techniques. Paradigm (sense 3) refers to the common training and socialization processes that Kuhn believes operate so as to bind scientists into a tightly knit community or communities with strong consensual norms.

As Masterman[28] points out, Kuhn often conflates these different meanings in his writing, so that 'paradigm' becomes a multi-purpose term roughly relating overall to the idea of a 'framework within which scientists are supposed to work'. Scientific training for Kuhn is supposed to involve the dogmatic initiation of trainee scientists into the 'normal science paradigm' in that they need to use textbooks which rarely if ever dwell upon the problematic nature of much scientific discovery, the personality of the discoverer and the social and political context in which the discovery is made. Instead, trainee scientists are led to believe that scientific progress is a-historic, a-personal and cumulative, each new discovery adding to the previously obtained body of knowledge. Socialization within the scientific community merely reinforces this view. As Kuhn points out, the scientific community could not function unless 'scientists fail to reject paradigms when faced with anomalies or counter-instances'.[29]

Paradigm (sense 3) referred to above is supposed by Kuhn to lead trainee scientists to become familiar with paradigms (senses 1 and 2) so that they may contribute to the reworking and refining of paradigms, an activity to which Kuhn refers as 'puzzle solving'[30] and on which he alleges scientists spend much of their time. All this is much to the disgust of Popper[31] who likes to think of scientists as 'problem solvers'[32] who can and do spend much of their time breaking out of their paradigms (senses 1 and 2), although as I noted earlier Popper has no way of showing how this 'break out' might be achieved.

It looks as if Kuhn is suggesting that scientific progress is made pragmatically by developing theories as responses to minor anomalies that show up from time to time. However, rather than its being the case that scientific progress is continuous, Kuhn is able to point out that the history of science is full of examples of long periods of 'normal science' broken by occasional periods of 'revolutionary science' that arise when scientists discover many anomalies within the normal science paradigm (sense 1). While it is always possible to accommodate an anomalous observation by slightly modifying the main paradigm (sense 1) (as I noted in my earlier discussion of Quine's work) and while it is also always possible to discredit or ignore the individual scientist who made the observation, (as Kuhn shows[33]) there are occasions when the number of occurrences of anomalies is so great that scientists start to feel under increasing psychological pressure and eventually attempt a 'mass break out' from the 'normal science paradigm'.

During these periods of 'revolutionary science', a number of alternative paradigms (1) and (2) are considered, each supported by various groups within the scientific community. Eventually a successor as chief paradigm (1) emerges from the competing paradigms and a new period of 'normal science' begins. Kuhn maintains that the new and old paradigms are now radically 'incommensurable' in the sense that the same words in each of them are used in a completely different way after a period of 'revolutionary science'. He writes: 'after a revolution, scientists work in a different world'.[34] This argument makes it look as if scientific progress is dependent upon the psychology of individual scientists; in this way Kuhn's earlier work may be regarded as a kind of sociology of the scientific community rather than an account of the logic of scientific discourse. Furthermore, the same argument is circular since two particular sciences (psychology and sociology) are supposed to hold the key to the way that all sciences function.

In *The Essential Tension*[35] Kuhn attempts to takes account of some of the criticisms of his earlier work by incorporating some demarcation criteria within his elitist philosophy of science. Kuhn now agrees with his critics that such standard criteria as accuracy, simplicity, coherence, breadth and predictive power 'provide the shared basis for theory choice'.[36] Nevertheless, for Kuhn, these criteria can never determine theory choice nor can they ever be explicitly stated and applied, because of the indeterminacy of interpreting these or any other criteria. Instead, Kuhn suggests that such criteria function as values that guide scientific communities.

For Kuhn, there will always be debate about the ways in which particular theories should be judged but that does not make theory preference a matter of 'taste'. Instead, Kuhn recognizes that, in so far as theories can be said to exist, theories exist in use. That is to say, theories are put forward, justified and compared by members of a community who are guided by certain values and who agree on particular ways of describing the world that are assumed by those theories. That is not to say that such agreement is uniform. Rather it is to say that there are overlapping ways of using scientific terms that make it possible for the proponents of rival scientific theories to interpret what each other is doing.

Hence, for Kuhn, theory choice becomes a matter of translation of ideas and statements between the proponents of different theories. Their shared commitment to the previously mentioned values is sufficient to ensure that the effort of translation is worthwhile.

> However incomprehensible the new theory may be to the proponents of tradition, the exhibit of impressive concrete results will persuade at least a few of them that they must discover how such results are achieved. For that purpose they must learn to translate, perhaps by treating already published papers as a Rosetta stone or, often more effective, by visiting the innovator, talking with him, watching him and his students at work. Those exposures may not result in the adoption of the theory; some advocates of the tradition may return home and attempt to adjust the old theory to produce equivalent results. But others if the new theory is to survive, will find that at some point in the language-learning process they have ceased to translate and begun instead to speak the

language like a native. No process quite like choice has occurred, but they are practising the new theory nonetheless.[37]

This argument is important because it helps us to begin to link theoretical and practical interest. For example, we may extend the argument to explain both the attraction and the failure of recent attempts made by some educational theorists to emulate natural scientific methodology. These educational theorists may be seen to be attracted to what they assume to be natural scientific methodology for the reason that they too are attracted by the 'exhibit of impressive concrete results'. However, by characterizing natural science as from within the paradigm of foundationalist empiricism, these educational theorists have been attempting to emulate the activities of those who use procedures that are not part of natural scientific methodology and hence are not likely to exhibit the 'impressive concrete results' that are commonly assumed to be produced by natural scientists.

This argument may also be extended to explain why 'scientific' societies may be considered to be more rational than primitive societies. I refer to the literature concerned with the issue of the 'rationality' of the Azande.[38] In the course of a discussion on this, Winch[39] criticizes Evans-Pritchard for holding that 'his' standard of rationality can enable him to deem Zande belief in witches to be irrational. However, Winch points out that Evans-Pritchard speaks from

> a culture whose conception of rationality is deeply affected by the achievements and methods of the sciences and one which treats such things as a belief in magic or the practice of consulting oracles as almost a paradigm of the irrational.[40]

Consequently Winch holds that Zande beliefs and actions may only be appraised against and within Zande 'forms of life'.

Other writers, by contrast, argue that Western European 'forms of life' are more rational than those of the Azande and that this is because of the achievements of the natural sciences. For example, Gellner writes:

> The importance of . . . the scientific industrial 'form of life' whose rapid global diffusion is the main event of our time, is that it does provide us with a solution to the problem of relativism . . . The cognitive and technological superiority of one form of life is so manifest and so loaded with implications . . . that it simply cannot be questioned.[41]

Taylor[42] too argues that trans-cultural judgments of rationality can be made on the basis of the supposed superiority of a theoretical culture over an a-theoretical one because the former effectively lays out the way the world is with a perspicuity that commands the attention of the latter both intellectually and by way of its technological applications.

Taylor does not suggest that the Azande are less rational because they believe in magic or consult oracles. He accepts that such beliefs and practices are incommensurable with Western European ideas, the post-Enlightenment origins of which have tended to separate the notions of 'understanding' and 'attunement' through the ideal of scientific disinterest. Instead, Taylor suggests that the Azande are able to recognize the technological advances that result from the theoretical progress that the natural sciences have made. For example, the Azande may not understand the theory of vaccination but they certainly recognize the process of someone recovering from a fatal illness. To take another example, they may not understand the principle of the internal combustion engine but they certainly recognize the advantages that transport might afford them.

The argument may be put simply as follows: rationality depends upon theoretical understanding. Western European 'forms of life' support the enterprise of natural science. Natural science leads to technological control which commands the attention of non-scientific 'forms of life'. Therefore, Western European 'forms of life' are more rational than non-scientific 'forms of life'. Notice that this argument does not suggest that 'technological control' functions as a universal criterion of rationality that both Western Europeans and the Azande recognize. Nor does this argument suggest that the concept of rationality is completely circumscribed by theories about the natural world. It may be that in time certain features of Zande 'forms of life' may come to outweigh 'technological' considerations to bias judgments of rationality in favour of the Zande. However, despite radical incommensurabilities between 'scientific' and 'primitive' forms of life, trans-cultural judgments of rationality may be made in favour of the former because presently the former's technological control commands the attention of the latter in a way that outweighs any claims that the latter may make to command the attention of the former.

If Kuhn is correct in concluding that scientific theory preference can be explained by referring to the common values that bind the scientific community together and make it possible for scientists to interpret what each other is doing, then it follows that any group of theorists who share those values may also come to prefer some theories over others on the basis of their interpretations of what each other is doing. Just as natural scientists may interpret each other's work fruitfully so too other types of theorists may benefit by interpreting the work of natural scientists. Their interest might not quite coincide with the interest of the natural scientist, nevertheless there will be sufficient overlap to make interpretation possible. In other words, Kuhn's account of scientific theory preference may well be applied to any type of theory and especially educational theory if three things can be shown: first, that forms of discourse are commensurable — that is to say that the use of a term in one form of discourse is related to the use of a term in another; second, that the interpretation of those uses is no less complex for the natural scientist than it is for any other type of theorist; and third, that there are no categorical differences between theoretical and practical interests.

Commensurability

Let us begin by examining the notion of commensurability as it may be applied within natural science. The early Kuhn and Feyerabend's attack on commensurability lead to the idea that during periods of what Kuhn calls 'revolutionary science' the same words are used in completely different ways. However Putnam[43] argues against this idea. He argues that while the uses of scientific terms are continually changing, not all of their uses change at the same time. For example, Bohr's (1904) electron had a negative charge just as our present-day electron does, even though other properties may have changed. In this way Putnam seems to adopt a 'cluster' theory of reference in which the elements of a cluster are related by something like a 'family resemblance'. We can refer to Bohr's electron because we apply the 'principle of charity'.[44] We say in effect that there are sufficient common properties between the two 'electrons' to justify our calling them the same.

In order to use a scientific term intelligibly a speaker needs a standard minimum amount of information, something that Putnam calls a stereotype. Additionally a speaker needs some examples of extensions of the term. For example, speakers understand the term 'electron' if they have a stereotype which may consist of 'negative charge, small, part of an atom etc.', and some extensions of the term like 'Beta particle, present when current flows etc.'. Speakers do not need, nor could they have, all the extensions of a term because of the 'linguistic division of labour' thesis.[45] Putnam uses this phrase to draw attention to the social nature of language and the way in which the extensions of a term are divided among a community of speakers. Putnam puts it this way:

> Every linguistic community ... possesses at least some terms whose associated 'criteria' are known only to a subset of the speakers who acquire the terms, and whose use by the other speakers depends upon a structured cooperation between them and the speakers in the relevant subsets.[46]

The 'linguistic division of labour' thesis allows me to explain why Kuhn's earlier incommensurability thesis is implausible and why his earlier talk of scientists inhabiting 'different worlds'[47] is unhelpful. Since scientists do not all share the same extensions of terms and do not all shift allegiance from old to new paradigms at the same time, then scientific discourse reflects both old and new extensions of terms for some time after periods of 'revolutionary science'. Consequently linguistic practices that link new terms with old remain within the scientific community so that sense can be made of the idea of progress. That is not to say that one idea of progress governs all future ideas of progress. Rather it is that the idea of progress becomes, like the extensions of terms across the scientific community, spread across not only the scientific community but other communities as well, evolving with each change in linguistic practice. The Kuhnian incommensurability thesis is implausible precisely because speakers and communities of speakers do not remain in isolation from one another.

Let us now consider the notion of commensurability as it might apply across forms of discourse by making reference to Goodman's *Ways of Worldmaking*.[48] In Goodman's view it matters little whether we hold that there is a world of which it is possible to have a right version or whether we want to say that our versions are just our worlds, as long as we realize that what we say does not correspond with the world. Goodman suggests that we find the idea of multiple worlds unpalatable because we try to stretch the use of the word 'world' beyond its reach so that the world either becomes a fixed entity leading to utter resignation on our part as to the possibility of ever knowing it, or to 'irresponsible relativism'. Instead, Goodman suggests that we should accept a 'judicious vacillation' between worlds, rather like the physicist who

> flits back and forth between a world of waves and a world of particles. ... we are monists, pluralists, or nihilists not quite as the wind blows but as befits the context.[49]

The important point here is that the physicist's description of electro-magnetic radiation depends upon the way in which that description enmeshes with other forms of discourse in which the physicist engages. The physicist's use of the term 'wave' depends for its effectiveness upon a richness that is derived from a 'family resemblance' between the roles that the term plays in all forms of discourse in which that set of letters has meaning. The same may be said of other scientific terms. Hence scientific terms are not used in isolation from other forms of discourse, rather their scientific use is parasitic on non-scientific usage.

Rather than there being a privileged set of terms, for Goodman any set will do whether these are fundamental particles or everyday objects or even fictional entities. Thus, when we are asked to consider whether someone is a Don Quixote or a Don Juan, we find this question just as useful, and probably slightly easier to answer, as asking whether someone is paranoid or manic-depressive. Hence 'world-making' is not just the preserve of the scientist; the artist too makes worlds.

> When a scientist first relates heat to motion or the tides to the moon, our worldviews are drastically altered. And when we leave an exhibit of the works of an important painter, the world we step into is not the one we left when we went in, we see everything in terms of those works.[50]

Even though Goodman accepts that there are many 'right' ways of worldmaking, that does not mean that all 'right' alternatives are equally good for every purpose. Instead, we need to construct 'right' versions for particular purposes. These versions may involve extensional logic, fundamental particles, or paintings. In Goodman's view, a 'right' version cannot be grounded in any context-free way.

We may then have different 'versions' of the 'world' and each version can be 'right' in the sense that a 'right version' maximizes 'the cogency and the compactness and comprehensiveness, the informativeness and organizing power of the whole system'.[51] 'Rightness' is primarily a matter of 'fit' — fit is what is referred to in one way and another; goodness of fit is limited by all sorts of things, including deductive rightness, inductive rightness and rightness of categorization. For example:

> Whether a picture is rightly designed or a statement correctly described is tested by examination and reexamination of the

picture or statement and what it refers to by trying its fit in varied applications and with other patterns and statements.[52]

Hence theories are not only to be understood as constituent parts of one form of discourse, but also are related to all forms of discourse through a process of gradual adjustment brought about by the use of their terms in different contexts. The richness of meaning of both scientific and non-scientific terms depends upon family resemblances between them and our rationality depends upon our ability and willingness not to try to find one form of discourse to which all others are supposed to relate but rather to be open-minded enough to challenge all of our preconceptions by continuing to place features of various forms of discourse in temporary 'cosmic exile' while the coherence of the rest of our theoretic network is increased.

Quine's 'seamless web' may thus be made up of all kinds of material. Yet it is not hard to envisage some overall theoretical web within which a variety of forms of discourse constantly shift into the most coherent arrangement, both on the basis of theories about the sorts of lives that people want to lead and on the basis of those theories that have the most empirical content. The upshot of all this discussion is that there are not likely to be any significant differences between various means of preferring any particular type of theory. Theory preference is always under-determined by 'experience' and so 'value' considerations must be taken into account in order to enable us to determine theory choice in the concrete instances in which such choices are made. In the next section, I argue that the values that Kuhn suggests are the guides to natural science may themselves be filtered out over time according to the way in which a variety of discourses enmesh.

Theory and Practical Interest

It is widely accepted[53] that there is a three-way relationship operating in both natural and social sciences between the objects of study, the scientist, and the scientific community. In each case the scientist communicates the regularities about the object of study he claims to have isolated to the scientific community of which he is a member. However, in the case of the natural scientist the only communication that takes place is that between the scientist and his colleagues in his scholarly community; this presupposes only one interpretive dimension. For the social scientist, by contrast, there are two kinds of communication: that which takes place between the scientist and the objects of study (people), and that which takes place between the social scientist and his colleagues in his community. This presupposes two interpretive dimensions; this is sometimes referred to as the 'double hermeneutic'[54] operating in the case of the social science.

The 'double hermeneutic' seems to impose on the social scientist the joint requirement — and the double problem — of being both a part of the object of study as well as a member of a community of fellow social scientists. Social scientists aim to provide an account of the objects of study that satisfies the rules of intelligibility and identity operating in the case of both the social scientific community and of the community being studied. In other words, it looks as if a social scientist should be a full member of both the social science community and of the community being studied. Furthermore, if the social scientist is a member and participant in both communities, the possibility of appraising beliefs or actions in one community as more or less rational than beliefs or actions in another community seems to be excluded.

Suppose, for example, that a social scientist wishes to investigate the effect of astrology on the lives of a particular group of people who regularly consult horoscopes and in some way adjust their lives accordingly. Suppose as well that the social scientist considers that it is irrational to believe in the findings and recommendations of astrology. How can the social scientist understand those for whom astrology is important and for whom it is regarded as rational to consult horoscopes? Only, according to Winch[55] and others, by entering the 'form of life' of the astrology believers. But this is impossible. The 'disinterested' (if such a position is possible) social scientist simply cannot identify instances when astrology is important for people because such a possibility is ruled out *a priori* for him; and pretending that astrology is important cannot help him.

Such a move effectively puts an end to the idea of a 'social science'. The move is therefore commonly resisted on the grounds *inter alia* that it would also put an end to the idea that theoretical understanding is a necessary underpinning for rationality. Such a move would rule out the possibility of social theorists claiming some special status for their contributions to debates on the social controls and pressures that might be brought to bear in a particular conflict between interested parties in a plural society.

In order to resist this move, Giddens suggests that social scientists should develop a technical meta-language that serves both to distinguish the activity of the social scientist from that of lay-actor and serves to account for the superiority of the former's theoretical output. This move seems to support the view that the social sciences should follow the model of the natural sciences, but Giddens stresses that social sciences have to deal with an additional frame of meaning not present in the natural sciences and involving the 'double hermeneutic'. As he puts it:

> Any generalized theoretical scheme in the natural or social sciences is in a certain sense a form of life in itself, the concepts of which have to be mastered as a mode of practical activity generating specific types of descriptions ... Sociology, however, deals with a universe which is already constituted within frames of meaning by social actors themselves, and reinterprets these within its own theoretical schemes, mediating ordinary and technical language.[56]

In this way Giddens seems to suggest that natural scientific discourse is set apart from ordinary discourse: the only interpretive dimension relevant to the work of the natural scientist is that involving his interpretation of the work of other natural scientists. However, I think that Giddens is mistaken in his apparent assumption that natural scientific discourse is any more 'all of a piece' than, say, a combination of sociological and ordinary discourse. As I argued, the language of theoretical science is no less 'metaphorical and unformalisable'[57] than ordinary language. Moreover, the very broad distinction within natural science between the experimental and theoretical communities involves a member of the 'theoretical' community interpreting both the work of his theoretical colleagues and the work of the 'experimental' community. The same may be said for a member of the 'experimental' community. Now this very broad distinction within natural science may be likened to the distinction between social scientist and ordinary person. Just as the theoretical physicist has to interpret what his experimental colleagues are saying, so the social scientist has to interpret the ordinary language of the person, as well as interpreting what his own theoretical colleagues are saying.

It may well be, as Giddens argues, that there is 'considerable complexity'[58] in the case of the sociologist/person relationship that is not so obvious in the case of the theoretical/experimental physicist relationship. Nevertheless this 'complexity' makes the difference between natural and social sciences one of degree rather than kind. Giddens also argues that:

there is a continual 'slippage' of the concepts constructed in sociology, whereby these are appropriated by those whose conduct they were originally coined to analyse, and hence tend to become integral features of that conduct (thereby in fact potentially compromising their original usage within the technical vocabulary of social science).[59]

Now we have no reason to suppose that this 'slippage' is any more a feature of social science than of natural science. Yet such 'slippage' may be much more obvious or apparent in social science because social science is so closely connected with ordinary forms of discourse and the interests that such discourse reflects.

As I have already argued, there is a 'linguistic division of labour' at work across the scientific community that brings it about that scientific communication is only partial and that there are many interpretive dimensions relevant to the choice of theories that the community makes. In particular, the notion of the possibility of theory-preference depends upon the range, richness and functional utility of those metaphors that are theoretically situated — a richness that is itself dependent upon the ways in which terms from a variety of forms of discourse come to interact.

However, even if it were accepted that there are many interpretive dimensions relevant to theory preference in natural and social science (such that natural scientific discourse is no more 'all of a piece' than social scientific discourse) and even if it were accepted that theory in both cases were under-determined by data, it could still be argued that those interests that determine theory preference in natural scientific theory are different from those that determine theory preference in social scientific theory. It might be argued that the natural scientific interests of simplicity, coherence, scope and so on, are of a different kind from the practical interests that might determine which of two rival educational theories are to be preferred, for example.

Implicit in this view is the distinction between interests that are theoretical and impersonal, and those that reflect the personal commitments that a theoretical account is regarded as intended to transcend. However, just because natural scientific theory is not so obviously related to immediate human concerns as educational theory, which might imply practical recommendations, is no reason to suppose that the latter type of theory might not be guided by the same interests as the former type. Nor is there any reason to suppose that the natural scientific interests of simplicity, coherence and so on, do not imply practical recommendations for the natural scientist that guide the way that he conducts the professional part of his life.

Instead, the distinction between practical and theoretical interests might be more a matter of degree of commensurability with immediate human concerns rather than a difference in kind. For example, Hesse argues that in natural science there is an overarching pragmatic criterion that 'filters out both simplicity criteria and other value judgements'.[60] Hesse is not arguing for a new form of pragmatism; she simply avers that presently we can make sense of the idea of increasing predictive success. As she puts it:

> The spaceship still goes whether described in a basically Newtonian or relativistic framework.[61]

This might be taken to mean that both frameworks are useful devices for predicting the movement of spaceships and that the pragmatic criterion can be seen to be applicable to both frameworks despite their radical conceptual differences internally.

> There are notorious difficulties ... that underlie the notions of underdetermined theories and criticisms of the basic observation language. The pragmatic criterion trades these difficulties for others by bypassing the question of the reference of theoretical language, and resting on the non-linguistic concept of successful prediction.[62]

However, it is difficult to understand what Hesse means by the idea of a 'non-linguistic concept'. She does not seem to mean that such a concept is transcendental since she goes on to argue that this concept could in time be replaced. Perhaps she means to suggest that the replacement of the pragmatic criterion would not come about simply as a result of modifications to natural scientific discourse but rather as a result of a complex rearrangement of a variety of forms of discourse including ethics.

For example, it could be argued that the enhanced status of the natural sciences results from successful technological applications of them. It could be argued that the explanatory and predictive success of natural scientific theories are of less concern to most people than their technological applications. Just as the traditional practices of building and farming command our attention because of the way that they afford us shelter and food, so too it could be argued that natural science commands our attention because of the way that natural science affords us mains electricity, washing machines and so on.

However, events such as those that took place at Chernobyl and Three Mile Island tend to shake our belief in the idea of progress based on natural science. These events tend to make us reassess the kind of world we want to inhabit and, while the resulting ethical discussion does not directly bear upon the values that guide the natural scientific community, such discussion does have perturbations across a range of forms of discourse and the precise formulation of the pragmatic criterion, that Hesse suggests 'filters out' other values, itself shifts. To an extent we may imagine that certain forms of discourse are legitimated by appeals to the claimed pragmatic benefits that are obtained from their application, though this is not a straight-forward appeal to immediate utility. Instead, such appeals are mediated by the way in which they enmesh with other appeals from other forms of discourse, some of which are concerned with speculations about the sort of world that we want to inhabit — in other words, with axiological considerations.

The picture that I am suggesting is one of a developing network of theories whose theory extensions are not only governed by observation statements but also by axiological considerations which, through a process of 'filtering' across many forms of discourse, come to function as values that guide various communities of theorists. The proximity of their theoretical concerns with our ethical discussions is a matter of degree but does not give rise to any clear distinction between so-called theoretical and practical interests.

According to this view, there is no reason for theories, in which a particular interest is apparent, to be any less informative and useful than those where personal interest is less apparent. Even minimally articulated, social theories can illuminate aspects of our lives despite the interests of their proponents. The question is, how can such illumination come about? How can an account that is 'interested', and in that way 'prejudiced', possibly illuminate our choices about what we might do? In order to answer these questions I turn in the next chapter to Gadamer's account of hermeneutics.

In this chapter we have moved beyond objectivism and relativism to see how Kuhn's account of natural science offers the possibility of accounting for the way in which a theoretic network that includes various types of theory might develop according to the ways in which the proponents of rival theories interpret what each other is doing. We have seen how natural science may be considered to be made up of subsets of speakers and we have seen how the idea of the linguistic division of labour thesis within natural science must be applied to other forms of discourse in order to account for linguistic practice within science.

The overall view that emerges is of a theoretic network that is supported by a variety of linguistic communities whose memberships, practices and evaluative concerns overlap, making the effort of interpretation both worthwhile and possible. Moreover it is during the process of interpretation that the use of a term in one form of discourse acts as a 'touchstone' for its use in other forms of discourse. We may achieve the opportunity of temporary 'cosmic exile' from our developing network of theory by continuing to place each of our preconceptions in jeopardy while our developing theoretic network is rearranged.

Notes and References

1   cf. BERNSTEIN, R.J. (1983) *Beyond Objectivism and Relativism*.
2   cf. LAKATOS, I. (1978) *Mathematics, Science and Epistemology* pp. 110–20.
3   The notion of 'professional judgment' is important here as it is this notion to which an appeal is often made finally to settle a dispute, as for example in the cases of a teacher's assessment of a student's aptitude for a particular course or a doctor's assessment of a patient's suitability for a particularly expensive operation.
4   QUINE, W.V.O. (1960) *Word and Object*, p. 235.
5   cf. WILSON, B.R. (Ed.) (1970) *Rationality*; HOLLIS, M. and LUKES, S. (Eds) (1982) *Rationality and Relativism*.
6   WINCH, P. (1964) 'Understanding a primitive society' reprinted in WILSON, B.R. (1970); and WINCH, P. (1972) *Ethics and Action*, pp. 8–49, see especially pp. 19–21.
7   QUINE, W.V.O. 1960, ch. 2; and QUINE, W.V.O. (1969) *Ontological Relativity and Other Essays*, ch. 1.
8   PUTNAM, H. (1978) *Meaning and the Moral Sciences*, pp. 41–50.
9   See HESSE, M. (1980) 'Habermas's consensus theory of truth', pp. 206–35, in her *Revolutions and Reconstructions in the Philosophy of Science*.
10 cf. HABERMAS, J. (1984) *The Theory of Communicative Action*, Vol. 1, p. 8.
11 This tension arises because of Popper's advocacy of bold conjecture in the field of natural science and his advocacy of piecemeal approaches in the field of social philosophy. See his *The Poverty of Historicism*, 1961, and *The Open Society and its Enemies*, Vol. II, 1945.
12 Popper argues that bold social experimentation would require great social control. However, social control limits the scientific freedom to reject failed experiments. Therefore the methodology of conjecture and refutation can only be applied piecemeal to social science.
13 LAKATOS, I., 1978, ch. 2.

14   WITTGENSTEIN, L. (1953) *Philosophical Investigations*, p. 60.
15   RIZVI, F. (1983) *The Fact-Value Distinction and the Logic of Educational Theory*, p. 58.
16   WITTGENSTEIN, L. 1953, p. 81.
17   KRIPKE, S. (1982) *Wittgenstein: On Rules and Private Language*.
18   This is usually taken to commence at P.I. 243. However Kripke argues that the solution to the paradox has already been given in the section that precedes P.I. 243.
19   This 'move to practice' in education may be seen to be exhibited by BARROW, R. (1984) *Giving Teaching Back to Teachers*; by CARR, W., some of whose publications are given in the Bibliography and whose work is discussed in Chapter 5; by RIZVI, F., 1983; by WALKER, J. and EVERS, C.W., again see the Bibliography for a list of some of their publications.
20   HIRST, P.H. (1983) 'Educational theory' in HIRST, P.H. (Ed.) *Educational Theory and its Foundation Disciplines*, p. 28.
21   Hirst adopts Oakeshott's distinction between 'technical' knowledge that can be formulated in propositions and 'practical' knowledge that exists only in use. See his *Rationalism in Politics*, 1962. See also POLANYI, M. (1958) *Personal Knowledge*, whose notion of 'tacit' knowledge has won some support in attempts to account for the apparent ability for people just to act intelligently but unreflectively. According to Polanyi people are supposed to share a common interpretive framework that is not stable but is simply shared by those working within it. For a discussion of some implications that Polanyi's work might have for educators, see BROWNHILL, R.J. (1983) *Education and the Nature of Knowledge*.
22   HIRST, P.H., 1983, p. 21.
23   *Ibid*.
24   This term is a main feature of the 'National Vocational Qualifications'. It is meant to define the standards of practical performance to which students should aspire.
25   KUHN, T.S. (1962) *The Structure of Scientific Revolutions*.
26   KUHN, T.S. (1977) *The Essential Tension*.
27   Kuhn concedes this point in his 'Logic of discovery or psychology of research?' in LAKATOS, I. and MUSGRAVE, A. (Eds) (1970) *Criticism and the Growth of Knowledge*, pp. 1–24.
28   MASTERMAN, M. (1970) 'The nature of a paradigm' in LAKATOS, I. and MUSGRAVE, A. (Eds) 1970, pp. 59–91.
29   KUHN, T.S., 1962, p. 78.
30   KUHN, T.S., 1970, p. 4.
31   I alluded to this distinction between 'puzzles' and 'problems' in connection with my earlier discussion of pragmatism.
32   POPPER, K.R. (1970) 'Normal science and its dangers', in LAKATOS, I. and MUSGRAVE, A. (Eds) 1970, p. 54.
33   KUHN, T.S., 1962, p. 78.
34   *Ibid*., p. 135.
35   KUHN, T.S., 1977.
36   *Ibid*., p. 322.
37   *Ibid*., p. 339.
38   see WILSON, B.R. (Ed.) 1970; and HOLLIS, M. and LUKES, S. (Eds) 1982.

39 WINCH, P., 1972.
40 *Ibid.*, p. 9; also in WINCH, P., 1972.
41 GELLNER, E. (1973) *Cause and Meaning in the Social Sciences* p. 87.
42 TAYLOR, C. (1985) *Philosophical Papers 2*, especially pp. 134–51.
43 PUTNAM, H. 1978, p. 58.
44 *Ibid.*, p. 22.
45 PUTNAM, H. (1975) *Mind Language and Reality*, pp. 227–9.
46 *Ibid.*, p. 228.
47 KUHN, T.S., 1962, p. 120.
48 GOODMAN, N. (1978) *Ways of Worldmaking*.
49 GOODMAN, N. (1984) *Of Mind and Other Matters*, pp. 32–3.
50 *Ibid.*, p. 192.
51 GOODMAN, N., 1978, p. 19.
52 *Ibid.*, p. 139.
53 cf. WINCH, P. (1958) *The Idea of a Social Science*.
54 GIDDENS, A. (1976) *New Rules of Sociological Method*, p. 158.
55 See WINCH, P. (1964) 'Understanding a primitive society', reprinted in
    WILSON, B.R., 1970, and WINCH, P. (1972) *Ethics and Action* pp. 8–49, p.
    43 in that collection. Winch seems to be unable to account for the way in
    which people from different 'forms of life' might come to understand
    what each other is doing. However, he avoids this difficulty by noting
    that while the social scientific community and the astrology believers
    disagree about astrology, they share what Winch calls 'limiting notions'.
    These are notions that all humans share regarding such biological
    universals as birth, death and sexual relations. These 'limiting notions'
    are supposed to give us the basic purchase required on the enterprise
    of understanding each other.
        However, it is inter-cultural as opposed to intra-cultural actions that
    present the most important occasions for social scientific analysis and
    enquiry. For example, for some social scientists an analysis of Zande
    witchcraft may well be interesting but less important than an analysis of
    soccer hooliganism or mugging. Winch treats such instances as 'cultural-
    ly situated' and hence conventional. Furthermore, 'limiting notions'
    cannot serve to determine which account of a social phenomenon is to
    be preferred from among a multitude of possibilities. Winch's problem
    is that he wants to work out a way in which ordinary language can be
    used to redescribe ordinary language and so gets caught up in the
    familiar difficulty for Wittgensteinians (see my Chapter 1) — that of
    accounting for the alleged superiority of any one form of discourse over
    others.
56 GIDDENS, A., 1976, p. 162.
57 cf. HESSE, M. (1980) *Revolutions and Reconstructions in the Philosophy of
    Science*, p. 173.
58 GIDDENS, A., 1976, p. 162.
59 *Ibid.*
60 HESSE, M., 1980, p. 190.
61 *Ibid.*, p. 192.
62 *Ibid.*, p. 193.

Chapter 5

Hermeneutics

In the previous chapter I argued that the question of accounting for
theory preference in the natural sciences involves the proponents of
rival theories interpreting what each other is doing according to those
values that are shared by members of the natural scientific community. I also argued that the members of a community of educational
theorists might be sufficiently attracted by the results of those interpretive procedures within natural science that they attempt to emulate
them when theorizing about education. I argued that this emulation is
possible because there are no significant interpretive differences between natural scientific and any other type of theory, nor are there
any differences in kind between theoretical and practical interests.
These arguments were intended to establish my thesis that our
theories and practices are bound together in the same network and
that the extent of the coherence of that network is an indicator of our
rationality. In this chapter I discuss the educational implications of
Gadamer's account of hermeneutics in an attempt to show how theory
and practice can be fused in the notion of a conversation. I go on
briefly to discuss Habermas's criticisms of Gadamer's work as these
criticisms relate to educational theory. I conclude by offering a critique of the action research movement as it arises out of Habermas's
work.

Post-empiricist philosophers of science may be thought to have
moved the focus of the problem of the theory-laden nature of
observation statements back to the problem of the value-laden nature
of all theory. In the first case, the idea that the identification of
falsifying instances depends upon an overall understanding of the way
in which a network of theories fits together seems to be prime. In the
second case, the notion of dependence upon a common commitment
to certain values on the part of all theorists is a dominant *motif*. But

both share the pre-conception that our selection or rejection of a particular theory depends upon our having some sort of prior under-standing of the 'scientific'/theoretic enterprise, that has already in a sense determined our selection or rejection. But it also leads to vicious circularity within scientific discourse.

Hermeneutics, conceived as the study of the problem of the possibility and intelligibility of our attempts to give an interpretation and achieve understanding, contains its own 'critical circle'[1] that is supposed to avoid that kind of viciousness. According to Heidegger:

> Any interpretation which is to contribute understanding must already have understood what is to be interpreted.[2]

What Heidegger means is that, in order for us to interpret part of the behaviour of a community, we need to understand the way that the part we are concerned to analyze ralates to the overall way that a community lives. The opposite is also true: in order to understand the whole, it is necessary to understand the various constituent parts. To take another example; in order to convince people of the 'correctness' of an interpretation, we need to assume that they understand what is being interpreted in the same way as we do. If they do not, then all we can do is to try to interpret other expressions in the hope that we shall convince them of the suitability or appropriateness of our inter-pretation. However, at bottom, Taylor points out:

> We cannot escape an ultimate appeal to a common understand-ing of the expressions, of the 'language' involved.[3]

So if we cannot convince someone else of our 'correct' interpretation, then there may well arise doubt about our own supposedly correct interpretation. The hermeneutic 'circle' is therefore 'critical', in the sense that its adoption involves the constant questioning of one's own presuppositions and interpretations.

This apparent circularity is not vicious, however, since it is actually presupposed in every act of understanding. Again according to Heidegger:

> if we see this circle as a vicious one and look out for ways of avoiding it, even if we just 'sense' it as an inevitable imperfec-tion, then the act of understanding has been misunderstood from the ground up ... What is decisive is not to get out of the circle but to come to it in the right way. This circle of

understanding ... is not to be reduced to the level of a vicious circle, or even of a circle which is merely tolerated. In this circle is hidden a positive possibility of the most primordial kind of knowing.[4]

For Heidegger, the circularity is not only present in the understanding of others but also when we reflect upon what we ourselves do. The hermeneutic circle provides us with a means of attaining a reflective kind of self-understanding that is an essential part of being human.

The following example may illustrate this point: recently there have been some investigations into the possibility of a causal connection between levels of radiation and childhood cancers. The empiricist suppositions of some investigators rightly led them to be cautious in drawing conclusions that such a causal connection exists.[5] Statistical probabilities were quoted and there was mention of increased counselling for parents who might be worried. All this seemed a sane and reasonable response to many people. Yet when asked to imagine what he would do if his own family were exposed to these risks, the chief investigator stated that he would remove them from the risk despite the financial and other losses that their removal might incur. By self-reflection, the investigator came to know what he might do. Knowing subject and object under investigation were fused in that imaginary instance — the circularity that is endemic to empiricism was transcended. We should not expect this kind of knowing to lead to universal decisions, nor should we expect our predicament to be systematically resolved as if by continued reflection we come to know things as they really are.

Gadamer's Hermeneutics

Originally hermeneutics was concerned with understanding what was problematic about the meaning of certain religious and historical texts. Schleiermacher[6] and Dilthey,[7] working in accordance with the ideals of the Enlightenment, attempted to transcend the distortions inherent in accounts influenced by an interpreter's own tradition, in the attempt to produce a 'correct' or the 'definitive' interpretation by constant application of a particular 'impersonal' method. Gadamer follows Heidegger in attempting a different project for hermeneutics. Gadamer is not concerned to find one method of interpreting texts which will produce a 'once and for all' complete and correct interpretation. Indeed, he maintains that this is neither possible nor desirable. According to Gadamer hermeneutics is equally likely to affect the way that an interpreter sees his own immediate participation in a tradition, which itself influences the expectations which are brought to bear on a text as well as affecting the interpretation of the text itself.

Gadamer calls the effect of tradition 'prejudice' (*Vorurteil*)[8] and seeks to show in considerable detail how the Enlightenment deformed the use of the word 'prejudice' so that it now seems only to function in a pejorative way. Gadamer seeks to reinstate 'prejudice' as an essential part of the process of interpretation. Instead of searching to isolate and then elevate the idea of an a-temporal, bias-free interpretation, Gadamer acknowledges the essential temporality and prejudicial nature of our knowledge. As Linge puts it in the 'Introduction' to Gadamer's *Philosophical Hermeneutics*:

> The role of the past cannot be restricted merely to supplying the texts or events that make up the 'objects' of interpretation. As prejudice and tradition, the past also defines the ground the interpreter himself occupies when he understands.[9]

By substituting the words 'world' and 'experiment' for the words 'past' and 'interpretation' in the above quotation, we could easily read it as a statement of the problem of the theory-ladenness of observation statements. The words 'prejudice' and 'theory-laden' seem to perform complementary roles. The ease of such a proposed exchange reinforces my earlier point about the natural sciences also involving a hermeneutic dimension.

Since for Gadamer understanding is a temporal event in which a text is mediated by an interpreter's expectations or 'horizons' — and these in their turn are themselves mediated by the tradition which led to the original encounter between text and interpreter — interpretation is not something final but is a dynamic part of an ongoing conversation. Instead of there being one final interpretation or reconstruction, understanding consists of a series of mediations or 'fusing of horizons'[10] between interpreter and text. For Gadamer, interpretation, theorizing and application are all present in the moment of interpretation. The concept of understanding as a 'fusion of horizons' indicates that the horizons of the interpreter as well as the text change in the activity of seeking and coming to understanding; thus the interpreter's present situation is fluid, prejudices are continuously being discarded and reformed as a result of the understandings that we are constantly achieving and reconstructing. This puts an end to empiricist notions of what claims to be 'disinterested' educational research leading to theories that are applied in concrete practical situations.

The notion of a 'fusion of horizons' also puts an end to what I earlier called the professionalization of educational theory, that is to say, the process whereby educational theorists are assumed to be guardians of educational rationality (and as a result both claim and are offered enhanced institutional status including the right to the tutelage of teacher trainees). The present move to what is called 'the primacy of practice' that often results in the promotion of the notions of action research and action learning, may be seen to arise out of Gadamer's hermeneutics. On this basis we might claim that learning gets its moment of application in actual practice; for this reason we might think that so-called educational theorists should converse with so-called educational practitioners in order to enhance mutual understanding.

However, Gadamer's hermeneutics involves a more radical shift than this. It is not just that theory should be more related to practice or that theorists and practitioners should understand each other better: it is that there is no such thing as theory that is not itself a form of practice nor are there theorists who are not themselves practitioners or *vice-versa*. Crucially it makes no sense to imagine that there are theories to be had which guide practice. The radical thrust of Gadamer's hermeneutics applied to education today is to deny much of the present institutionalization of the 'theory guiding practice idea', whether that be in colleges and departments of education or colleges of further education providing the vocational theory that is supposed to guide vocational practice.

The idea that rational practice only results from successful theoretical deliberation should be rejected in favour of a view of practice that incorporates the constant mediation between talk about what to do next and action in the appropriate practical context. For example, the idea of a general vocational preparation needs to be tempered in favour of some form of apprenticeship system. If there are simply not enough jobs to go around, that is a problem but it is not an educational problem. One of the implications of Gadamer's hermeneutics is that our educational tradition should make us regard it as insufficient for the education system to be conceived primarily as the 'preparation' of people for an economic role in society and to be held primarily responsible for a society's failure to achieve its economic targets. It is much more reasonable to maintain, as M. Warnock[11] has argued, that education should be concerned both with a preparation for working life generally and with learning something about the ways in which different groups of people choose to live. No one totally shapes the society of which they are a part, any more than any one totally fits into it like a piece in a jigsaw puzzle.

The main educational implication of Gadamer's hermeneutics is that it challenges head-on the empiricist notion of a *tabula rasa*. It underlines the 'prejudicial' nature of all knowledge and the ways in which our cognitive prejudices are transformed through a continuous encounter with other prejudices. There may be no final rule or principle that governs the ways that our prejudices develop nor may there be any 'bits' of knowledge waiting to fill up any gaps in our conceptual scheme. Further, Gadamer enables and encourages us to account for the role that tradition plays in understanding and to criticize the idea that education is simply about transferring knowledge. The point is that knowledge is not a static piece of equipment or commodity just waiting to be 'slotted in' to some part of our cognitive apparatus where there is felt to be a conceptual deficiency, any more than an educand is a static commodity just waiting to be slotted into an economic deficiency. Instead, to come to know something is to have engaged in conversations in which one's prejudices have been transformed; as a result of such encounters and engagements one both acts and speaks differently.

Gadamer's notion of the mediation between text and interpreter can be seen as a dialogue involving equality and active reciprocity with 'prejudice' on both sides being discarded, as in a conversation between learners and teacher. Just as with a text that is interpreted, so a conversation is about something to which contributors direct their attention. The contributors do not, according to Gadamer, concentrate on each other's personality; rather they attempt to make each other's attempts at communication their own. It is imagination that enables the contributors to see what is questionable in the subjects of their conversation and to go beyond their original horizons in a process of enquiry that has in a very real sense a life of its own.[12]

Gadamer suggests that the phenomenology of the game may be a useful way of viewing a dialogue.

> When one enters into dialogue with another person and then is carried along further by the dialogue, it is no longer the will of the individual person, holding itself back or exposing itself, that is determinative. Rather the law of the subject-matter is at issue in the dialogue and that elicits statements and counter-statements and in the end plays them into each other.[13]

Playing a game involves a wholehearted commitment to the to-ing and fro-ing of the game. It involves taking a risk that frees the participants from their subjectivity and from the technicalities of the game. Similarly the contributors to a conversation do not already possess the language they use in any perfect or final sense. The selection of a word appropriate in any phase of the conversation is not made according to pre-given rules which the speaker possesses. Rather the meaning of the word is situation-dependent. The selection of a word is an act that in itself involves an infinity of possibilities which intrigue the participants into investigating ever new language situations.

This suggestion may help us to explain a situation with which most teachers and indeed most people are familiar. It is the situation in which a group of people seem so absorbed in what they are doing that questions of selection of appropriate strategy, control, management or technique are inappropriate. It is probably the most worthwhile and enjoyable learning situation yet its realization is almost certainly not the result of a psychological study of method, nor of refining technique in front of a video camera having followed a set of rules. Moreover, it seems obvious that present moves to increase what I earlier called managerialism are not likely to promote this situation either. Instead, the key ingredient appears to be mutual respect and a shared commitment within a group to explore fresh possibilities in an open and democratic way. Gadamer describes situations that are a long way from what I suspect many teachers will recognize as the rule-following, worksheet-completing mentality of many of our curricular policy-makers.

Gadamer's insistence on the importance of prejudice and his refusal to establish demarcation criteria for good 'prejudices' may be seen by some theorists of the objectivist persuasion to lead to relativism. After all, it might be argued, if learning is supposed to involve learners in conversation, how are they supposed to know what is right? We may respond that learners are not prisoners within their prejudicial frameworks which they have adopted by uncritical adherence to some authority, whether that authority is the authority of tradition as presented in textbooks and so on or the supposed authority of someone in power, like that of a teacher. Instead, learners are constantly modifying their prejudicial frameworks with every hermeneutic encounter, not just those that take place while at school. The more that learners risk their prejudices, the more likely it is that their frameworks will change.

Even given the provisional nature of our adherence to authority

— and despite the fact that our acceptance of authority may become associated in some minds with obedience to persons in positions of power — Gadamer still seeks to rid the notion of authority of what he considers to be its post-Enlightenment pejorative overtones. For Gadamer, the distinction between faith in authority and the use of reason has led some people to an erroneous belief that there is a distinction and a choice between either authority or reason; but just as authority is a source of prejudice so too is it a source of truth. Authority is a recognition of superior knowledge. While

> it is true that it is persons that have authority . . . the authority of persons is based ultimately not on the subjection and abdication of reason, but on recognition of knowledge — knowledge, namely, that the other is superior to oneself in judgement and insight and for this reason his judgement takes precedence.[14]

The validity of our claims to knowledge demands that one should give cognitive respect to the person in authority but their authority may be validated by other impersonal means, that is, by grounds based on reason. The recognition of authority in discourse serves as a device further to enable understanding. It is not as if every problematic knowledge claim has to be discursively validated; it can simply be accepted on the strength of the authority. Nor is it that a person is accepted as an authority across all fields of discourse; it is simply that authority, like prejudice, can be enabling.

This reinforces my earlier point about the interest-relativity of forms of explanation.[15] Sometimes an appeal to authority is all that is required to explain or justify a course of action but these appeals can only be effective if personal authority is recognized and not imposed. Such a recognition has implications both for the role of the teacher and for the role of the manager. Most teachers are well aware that their effectiveness depends upon their students having a respect for their authority and that might be why they may take great care in preparing the first few encounters with a class in order to establish the authority that they hope will sustain them through any subsequent mistakes they might make. I suggest that the talk of establishing good relationships in the classroom is a way of referring to problems to be solved on the way to securing recognition of the teacher's authority.

There is a further educational implication of Gadamer's discussion of the nature of authority. This is the one concerned with the authority of those who are paid to manage teachers in accordance with the kind of promotion structure that was discussed in Chapter 2. Authority, for Gadamer, can only be recognized and not imposed — and that means recognized by those whose actions are in some sense circumscribed by the authority. In other words, instead of having a promotion procedure that is 'top-down', in the sense that someone is appointed by people who occupy positions above the applicant in the promotion structure, in Gadamer's view it is people 'below' these higher managerial levels who should have a much greater say in promotion procedures based on the authority that they recognize.[16]

It seems obvious that some centralization of decision-making in education is both inevitable and necessary. However, just because someone's authority is recognized over a period of time is no reason to suppose that they will remain in authority forever nor that their authority is based on anything other than the respect of their colleagues. Instead, there would be much to be said in favour of fixed-term appointments, the termination of which would not be seen as a consequence of some sort of failure on the part of the incumbent but rather as a normal part of the way in which a community of educational practitioners goes about its business — a kind of institutionalized dynamism of authority transference and easement of change.

Much of the strong feeling that has recently been directed against proposals to strengthen the management of educational institutions[17] may be seen to have resulted from teachers perceiving an asymmetry between their own struggle to establish their authority with students and the apparent lack of question with which they are supposed to accept the authority of others. There may be a mismatch between the democracy of the classroom and a management structure that is perceived to be anti-democratic and this may be compounded by the difficulty of recognizing those people who are likely to command respect from their colleagues over a period of time. In this respect teachers are in a very difficult position for not only do bad appointments often lead to bad decisions that may set up inadequate organization and so make it even more difficult for teachers to establish their own authority, but teachers might be unable to do much about ameliorating such procedures other than continuing to do those things that might enable them to gain promotion, the gaining of which might not necessarily improve the authority they can hope to command from other unpromoted teachers.

Gadamer suggests an explanation as to how this problem might have arisen. His suggestion depends upon the reinstatement of the pre-Enlightenment notion of *praxis* which is practical knowledge of how to live.[18] According to Gadamer, *praxis* has become deformed into *techne* which is merely a skill or technique that can be learned and forgotten. He argues that by risking our own post-Enlightenment prejudices we come to see how the notion of practical knowledge has become equated with the means part of instrumental rationality. Instead, Gadamer maintains, both *praxis* and *techne* proceed in a dialectical relationship. This involves a constant mediation between knowledge and application; yet *praxis* involves the notion of some 'good' end — it is teleological. So while *praxis* has the dimension of a science in that it deals with some regularities, it is only achieved in its application. The characteristics of *praxis* also hold true for hermeneutics. By reflecting upon the possibilities of interpretation and understanding, understanding itself is enhanced. Gadamer draws the analogy as follows:

> understanding, like action always remains a risk and never leaves room for the simple application of a general knowledge ... understanding (like action) means a growth in inner awareness of future possibilities.[19]

Gadamer's hermeneutics involves a mediation of past and future horizons that is rooted in the experiences we have in the world. Hence hermeneutics is practical philosophy which

> vindicates again the noblest task of the citizen — decision-making according to one's own responsibility — instead of conceding that task to the expert.[20]

It follows from any acceptance of Gadamer's account by educators that debate about what to do in educational institutions must become a much more open process in which the notion of different groups of practitioners being circumscribed by different sorts of objectives is rejected in favour of the notion that the forms of discourse typical in education involve both evaluative and descriptive components and that these evolve according to the ways in which those forms of discourse interact. Since the Enlightenment, however, the 'theory guiding practice' idea has become so pervasive that some imagine that all practices are guided by our pre-existing epistemic and/or axiologic concerns and that all practice needs to be 'managed' similarly in the light of them. If we follow Gadamer we may give up not only this supposed distinction between normative and empirical theory but also those distinctions purported to subsist between theoretical and practical knowledge and between manager and teacher.

Instead we have a different starting point: theory and practice are fused within linguistic practices, that are themselves constantly being transformed. The only problem is that Gadamer does not suggest how one transformation is to be preferred to another; but he does not seem to see this as a problem, being content merely to argue that the pre-Enlightenment uses of certain terms are to be preferred. The nearest that he gets to a clarification and solution of this issue is to be found in his account of how it is that we judge works of art.

For Gadamer, in so far as our attention is engaged by a work of art, there is an interaction between spectator and work that is essential to the completeness of the work. It may be objected that if there is no one meaning or correct interpretation of a work of art and if art appreciation involves an individual encounter between person and work of art, then it looks as if we are caught up in a sophisticated form of evaluative relativism. However, Gadamer avoids this conclusion by drawing an analogy between the performance of a piece of music and our appreciating the plastic arts.

In order to perform a piece of music the performers must understand and interpret the score; similarly a sculpture needs to be interpreted. Now we often have no difficulty in judging good or bad performances, so why, asks Gadamer rhetorically, should we have any difficulty with judging works of art in general? If we are inclined to the view that objective judgment always involves an infallible algorithm or universal acclaim, then we shall be disappointed with Gadamer's explanation. This disappointment, however, may be avoided if we generalize Kuhn's account of normal and revolutionary science into what Rorty[21] calls normal and abnormal discourse. Just as natural science is supposed by Kuhn to depend on an 'essential tension' between tradition and innovation in scientific research, so Rorty supposes that, for a conversation to remain open, there must be an 'essential tension' between traditional or 'normal' discourse, in which there are accepted procedures for settling disagreement, and innovatory or 'abnormal' discourse, where such procedures do not exist.

Just as scientific communities agree in the language games they play, so too do farming, building, legal and many other types of community. What we know depends upon the networks of agreement within these communities and the contingency of meeting their members and of accepting and recognizing their authority. That is not to advocate relativism. No one believes that every member is equally competent nor that any account which might be offered is as good as any other. Our inability to justify moral claims, for instance, in an algorithmic way does not mean that such claims can never be settled.

Fairly obviously many moral claims are settled in ways that satisfy the claimants at the time of the claim. Of course those who the community recognizes as having superior competence in the areas of discourse within which the dispute is located are more likely to be able to support their claims than those whose competence is inferior but this ability is precisely what refutes emotivism and what stops any slide into (moral) relativism.

There appears to be a measure of agreement between Rorty and Gadamer in as much as Gadamer's notion of authority as the recognition of someone who knows can be understood as the recognition that someone is a full member of a 'normal' community. We do not have to be a full member of that community ourselves to recognize the authority nor do we have to be a full member of that community in order to cast doubts on its practices. All conversations share the characteristics of normal and abnormal discourse to varying degrees, depending on the amount of conceptual innovation involved. Abnormal discourse is related to normal discourse through 'family resemblances' that prevent hermeneutics from sliding into relativism. To put it in Gadamer's terms, the jettisoning of useless prejudice is made on the basis of a fusion of horizons. The horizon of expectation which a participant brings to an encounter is itself the result of the fusion of the many horizons that are rooted in normal discourse.

We may regard a 'fusion of horizons' as the risking of the prejudices of normal discourse in order to help us come to an understanding of what each other is saying. 'Risking' does not mean jettisoning them and the resultant abnormal discourse nevertheless has some things in common with normal discourse, for which accepted authorities and standards of adjudicating claims truth to exist. So it is the consensual norms and intersubjective meanings of the communities, of which the conversational partners are members, that sustain abnormal discourse and crucially keep the conversation going.

For the objectivist, however, this move is not acceptable. The problem is that both Gadamer and Rorty seem to take language itself as 'the given' and to rely on a form of 'decisionism' as the ultimate arbiter of linguistic practice transformation. That is to say, ultimately we just act, decide or prefer some transformations as opposed to others, and we go as far as we can in justifying those preferences — the content of our justifications depending upon the context in which a justification is required. Gadamer, in particular, does not seem to take account of the fact that power relations often operate in such a way as to deform not only the context in which a conversation takes place but also the language that the conversational partners use. For example, a meeting might be convened to formulate a particular curricular policy. In an ideal situation, all interested members of staff, students, parents and other persons could attend that meeting, argue their points of view and modify them in response to superior arguments. At the end of a prolonged discussion in which all points of view had been critically examined, a consensus would emerge.

However, all too often this process of coming to a consensus by the risking of prejudices in a wide ranging, open conversation is not realized. In the worst case, the chairperson has decided upon the outcome in advance of the discussion and has the power to manipulate the participants into agreement through control of their promotion prospects, their children's happiness at school or whatever. In other cases, participants may be intimidated by the meeting and hence they might refrain from arguing their case or from asking for clarification. It is not hard to see that a whole range of factors can prevent the realization of a context within which free open decision-making can take place.

There are further difficulties for a Gadamerian account of truth and moral discourse that are connected with the traditions that are embedded within the very language that the conversational partners use. In this book, for example, I am attempting to show that our theories and hence our language have become dominated (and in my view deformed) by a set of managerial power relations that cohere with objectivism. To do this I have tried to engage readers in a conversation that forces them to risk their existing prejudicial frameworks (where these incorporate objectivism etc.); I hope that this risk leads some readers to move beyond objectivism to an alternative account of rationality in education. In other words, I have had to extend ordinary language to reconstruct and bring into the open the process by which that language becomes distorted. The reconstruction is supposed to present a coherent narrative which results in the elimination of the distortions of which our ordinary language makes us bearers.

As far as I can see this critical project is consistent with Gadamer's hermeneutics. However, it is not hard to anticipate the principal objection raised by Habermas and others that Gadamer's work does not provide us with the means to rationally prefer one coherent narrative over another. After all, Habermas might argue that if all narratives are deformed in some way then how are we supposed to know which narrative is the least deformed. To answer that the least deformed narrative is the one that is most coherent with other attractive narratives only prompts the further question concerning the narrative that presents the most coherent account of coherence and so on. That is unless of course we follow Gadamer who confronts this question by linking the theoretical with the practical. It is not as if our lives consist of continuous theory comparison. Instead, theory and practice are fused through the notion of a prejudice for if we cannot understand something the answer may be to change ourselves. Wittgenstein's advice may be apposite:

> The way to solve the problem you see in life is to live in a way that will make what is problematic disappear.[22]

Habermas and Critical Theory

The literature that surrounds the term 'critical theory' is considerable.[23] Indeed, Habermas's individual contribution to this literature would occupy the assiduous reader for some considerable time.[24] It is not my intention to try to summarize that literature for this has been done in many places.[25] I do, however, want to bring out some of the similarities and differences between the hermeneutics of Gadamer and the more critical hermeneutics of Habermas. I believe that such a comparison reveals an important value that should guide our educational theories and practices.

Let us begin with the similarities: I think that Gadamer would agree with Habermas that as well as its role as a medium for understanding through the fusing of horizons

> Language is *also* a medium of domination and social force . . .
> Language is *also* ideological.[26] (original emphasis)

Even though Habermas seems to stress this negative aspect of language and to want a 'depth hermeneutics'[27] to transcend the actor's conversation and to re-orient the power relations that distort the language that conversational partners use, it is not clear that Habermas's appropriation of psychoanalytic theory is entirely inappropriate to Gadamer.

Habermas looks to psychoanalysis[28] to provide the model for the systematic reflection on language required by his version of a critical theory. As in psychoanalysis, where repressed motives and private needs can be reconstructed and brought out into the open in order to present a coherent narrative, which can be verified by the patient and which can result in the elimination of the distortions which the repressed motives and privatized needs have caused, so too critical theory seeks to reconstruct and bring into the open the events that take place and the process by which our ideology becomes distorted and to present a coherent narrative which results in the elimination of the distortions of which our language makes us bearers. In some ways psychoanalytic constructions are like hermeneutic accounts, in that interpretation must take the form of a translation into the lifeworld of the patient; but in other ways psychoanalytic constructions function as causal hypotheses, which can be corroborated only by the continuation of the patient's self-formation. That is to say, the patient's acceptance or denial of the construction is not sufficient in itself as decisive confirmation or falsification of the psychological construction.

There are, however, difficulties with the psychoanalytic/critical theory analogy. As Habermas himself points out, a precondition of the success of psychoanalysis is the patient's own desire to be helped, whereas critical theory is meant to reach people precisely because their distortions make them unable to see that they are suffering and need help. Furthermore, psychoanalysis sometimes involves temporarily prolonging a patient's suffering. It is hard to see how a critical theorist could prolong the suffering of some social group without having an institutionalized power to do so!

In reading Habermas one senses an impatience with the idea that all a critical theorist can do is to present a narrative that people either accept or not. Habermas seems to want to present a transcendental argument which 'grounds' criticism in some feature of the world. As others have noticed,[29] Habermas may be trying to find another form of objectivism. He is not content with the idea that criticism is necessarily partial[30] nor with Gadamer's insistence that all criticism presupposes a linguistic community.[31] For Gadamer, the attempt by Habermas to set aside *critique* of ideology apart from the hermeneutic circle is impossible.

Habermas's appropriation of psychoanalysis as an analogy seems to rest on the assumption that the analyst has some special insight not accessible to the analyzee, whereas Gadamer considers that the critic of ideology assumes a superiority for his insight that he cannot justify:

> the very ideal of reason forbids anyone to claim for himself the correct insight into another's delusion.[32]

For Gadamer, the analogy between psychoanalytical and sociological theory breaks down because of the impossibility of distinguishing between professional and communal relationships.

Where does the patient-relationship end and the social part-
nership in its unprofessional right begin? Most fundamentally:
over against what self-interpretation of the social consciousness (and all morality is such) is it in place not to enquire
behind that consciousness — and when is it not?[33] (original
emphasis)

The point is that normally the unconscious is the object of our
hermeneutic concern and, while the unconscious can be and is probed
in hermeneutic encounters and while the power of reflection seems
critically to examine our unconscious presuppositions, that is no
reason to suppose that an analyst has any 'correct' or 'final' or unique
insight into our individual consciousness or, as Habermas seems to
suppose, our 'collective' conscious appropriation of forms of language
that serve to conceal our 'true' or 'real' interests.

Habermas attempts to answer these criticisms in his *Theory of
Communicative Competence*.[34] In this he attempts to give a rational
reconstruction of the universal conditions of reason. The theory is
outlined below: communicative action, which includes speech as well
as non-verbal communication, requires a background consensus that
meets four claims: utterances must be intelligible; the propositional
content true; the performative component correct; and the acting
subject sincere. Whilst the satisfaction of each of these conditions can
be problematic, they can be redeemed in 'discourse'.

In discourse, the 'force' of the argument is the only permissible
compulsion . . . discourses do not compel their participants to
act . . . discourses produce nothing but arguments.[35]

The aim of discourse is to distinguish the challenged consensus from a
rational consensus, one that is attained when argument alone prevails.
This distinction does not appear to help us distinguish between distorted and undistorted communication, since action and discourse are
inevitably interwoven. However, Habermas supposes that

the design of an ideal speech situation is necessarily implied in
the structure of political speech, since all speech, even intentional deception is oriented towards the idea of truth. This idea
can only be analysed with regard to a consensus achieved in
unrestrained and universal discourse.[36]

Habermas aims to show that implicit in speech is the normative foundation of what discourse requires — that is, genuine symmetry between and among speech-partners, where no form of domination exists and argument alone prevails. In this respect Habermas seems to accept that the ideal speech situation exists as a counterfactual only. That is to say, Habermas does not suppose that such situations could ever be realized. Nevertheless he argues that we may always imagine the situation in which a group of people discuss what they should do with no concern other than that of coming to an agreement on the basis of argument alone and not on the basis of coercion, manipulative cleverness or personal preference. Consequently, he argues that we may always answer the question:

> How would the members of a social system, at a given stage in the development of productive forces have collectively and bindingly interpreted their needs ... if they could and would have decided on the organisation of social intercourse through discursive will-formation?[37]

Our answer to this question is supposed to enable us to select one interpretation of a social development in preference to others for the correct interpretation is the one given in our answer. The normative foundation of critical theory rests on the possibility that the ideal speech situation is inherent in the structure of social action which critical theory seeks to analyze. Hence anyone who participates in rational discourse cannot argue that non-discursive standards of rationality are just as good as their own. This argument, however, does not show that discursive rationality is universal. To show this Habermas has to attempt to show that the ability to reason argumentatively and reflectively about truth is a species-wide competence. If I am correct when I argue that objectivism is impossible, then we have good reasons to conclude that the theory of communicative competence amounts to no more than another attempt to present a narrative that engages us and has interesting implications for practice.

This conclusion takes us back towards Gadamer's hermeneutics. However, the notion of an ideal speech situation helps us to explain how theorizing can be something other than a mere pragmatic response to problems that arise. We noted that Popper's theory of truth as 'a regulative ideal to which a series of theories approaches asymptotically' leads to the mistaken conclusion that theory is exclusively concerned with 'puzzle solving' — eliminating 'minor anomalies' within a common framework of enquiry. If we substitute Habermas's consensus theory of truth based on 'the ideal speech situation' for Popper's correspondence theory of truth, we can explain 'revolutionary' changes in theory. Rather than imagining that consensus in an 'ideal speech situation' informs a *series* of theories, we may suggest that an 'ideal consensus' informs *each* attempt at theorizing. As Hesse puts it:

> Every theory making truth claims in a particular conceptual framework includes its own 'anticipations' of the total nature of the world as far as it is relevant to that theory. The commitment to anticipated consensus is the commitment to abandon falsified positions, and also to abandon conceptual schemes that do not lead to consensus. There is no last theory or theorist in the sense that science stops there frozen in whatever conceptual scheme happens to be then current. But every serious theory and sincere theorist is 'the last' in the sense that *that* is where the accountability in the face of ideal consensus operates for him. To enter the scientific community presupposes acceptance of that accountability.[38] (original emphasis)

In this way each attempt at theorizing may call into question either individual theories or a complete framework of enquiry and so each attempt at theorizing may lead to 'revolutionary' changes.

This explanation depends upon the assumption that an 'ideal consensus' should function like any other value judgment as a regulative principle that guides our theorizing. Put simply, our best theories and most propitious decisions are those that would command assent in situations that best approach the ideal described above. However, this assumption may be made only after an option is taken for practical discursive rationality rather than systems-theoretic rationality as a means of organizing social institutions. As Hesse notes:

> The choice of 'persons' and participatory meanings as fundamental concepts in the hermeneutical sciences is not a necessary choice, as is shown by Habermas's barely disguised fears that scientific and impersonal 'systems theories' may after all prove technically successful in organising post-capitalist society on a stable basis. The choice of the concept 'person' becomes 'transcendentally necessary' only *after* an option is taken for practical discursive rationality and individual humanity.[39] (original emphasis)

In other words, the alternative to the systems-theoretic approach of the empiricist is a form of practical rationality based on the 'ungrounded hope' that human life will be improved if theorists are guided by a concern to secure an 'ideal consensus'. At the end of the first phase of his work, Habermas expressed this 'hope' as follows:

> on this unavoidable fiction rests the humanity of intercourse of men who are still men.[40]

We should note, however, that the systems-theoretic approach of the empiricist cannot be 'grounded' either — this approach may be dominant simply because of the conservatism of those who happen to control institutional change. Habermas directs our attention to the important point that strategic action and theory-comparison might be interwoven. In other words, the dominance of objectivism may only be challenged by strategic action that embodies a practical discursive conception of rationality

Action Research

Recently the idea of 'action research' has been promoted partly as a reflection of a deep dissatisfaction with traditional empirical and interpretive approaches to educational research[41] but mainly as a challenge to the dominance of objectivism within education. W. Carr and S. Kemmis have given one of the best accounts of 'action research' that is underpinned by Habermas's work.[42] While I do not agree with some of Carr and Kemmis's conclusions, I believe that an examination of their work highlights an important problem for a hermeneutic conception of educational theory.[43]

Carr and Kemmis argue that action research

> emancipates teachers from their dependence on habit and tradition by providing them with the skills and resources that will enable them to reflect upon and examine critically the inadequacies of different conceptions of educational practice.[44]

They go on to elicit five defining characteristics of action research which may be summarized as follows:

1 Action research encourages equal participation and collaboration. So-called 'outsiders' are not part of the research process,

since they have no access to the practitioner's own meanings and may also distort the balance of equal participation. Carr and Kemmis lament that educational researchers of an empirical persuasion often call their work 'action research' in order to make it sound more acceptable to those who might be under investigation:[45]

> what passes for action research today is not action research at all, but merely a species of field experimentation or applied research carried out by academic or service researchers who co-opt practitioners into gathering data about educational problems for them.[46]

When this happens the outcomes are often technical rather than emancipating or practical.

2 Action research does not construe its object positivistically. Instead, its object is construed as *praxis* or 'personal knowledge', which is authenticated by rational reflection. The reflective process is viewed as a continuous spiral with teachers researching their own *praxis*.

3 Action research should involve methodical reflection in order to enable practitioners to distinguish between ideologically distorted interpretations and correct interpretations. Action researchers therefore need freedom of discourse in order to 'redeem validity claims'. They need open communication gained in actual experiences in order to engage in the

> selection of strategies, the resolution of tactics and the conduct of political struggle.[47]

4 The above requirements lead action researchers to identify what is wrong with the existing social order and particularly those aspects of it that frustrate their researches. Action researchers

> intervene critically in all patterns of action which fragment communities and isolate individuals ... This view of collaboration is the basis of social solidarity.[48]

5 Even though action research is directed by practice, it must 'relentlessly' pursue all aspects of irrationality, injustice and

domination and not rest content with small changes which merely 'anchor the conditions of the status quo'.[49]

Carr and Kemmis use the example of the way in which a school staff might set about implementing a programme for action research:

> the staff should have constituted itself so that its discourse was rational and authentic: so that people could speak openly and freely, so that (as individuals) they could understand what was being said (authenticity), and so that there would be mutual understanding through the language used (communication), and so that they could develop a common orientation towards action.[50]

As I pointed out earlier, however, to achieve this sort of constitution might not be possible within the legal and administrative framework presently laid down for schools to work within. For example, teachers are legally bound to a set of conditions of service that reflect and are entrenched within a hierarchical organizational structure. While promoted members of staff might be willing to relinquish their rights to certain privileges and salary differentials, they may not be able to relinquish their rights to pension differentials and their legal responsibilities for the efficient running of the school. The present legal framework may preclude the constitution of an 'action research' community *ab initio* and the discourse of those communities that purport to be constituted as above, in fact might be systematically distorted.

Even if these legal and administrative problems could be overcome, Carr and Kemmis recognize that

> as real decisions are taken, the self-interests of some of the staff will be served at the expense of the self-interests of others, and self-interests of the staff may come into conflict with self-interests outside the group (those of students and parents, for example).[51]

The real problem here is that there are other individuals interested in the educational enterprise, as well as teachers, and it may be that these other individuals need to be emancipated from their inadequate conceptual frameworks. By construing 'educational theory' exclusively as a response to the problems that teachers face, Carr and Kemmis lack any means of knowing just whose conceptual framework is inadequate and to what extent it is inadequate. It will not do to imagine that the activity of teachers incorporating the notions of *praxis* and open communication will make it obvious to all which problems are to be tackled first and by whom.

Were the main focus of attention for 'action research' to be classroom practice, then it might not matter so much that Carr and Kemmis construe action research as a response to the problems that teachers face. As it is, however, Carr and Kemmis are keen to avoid limiting the scope of action research in this way.[52] Yet if action researchers are to move beyond classroom research and to 'reject all conditions which sustain irrationality, injustice and domination'[53] then it follows that teachers as 'action researchers' should be able to recognize when such conditions arise. However, this conclusion begs both the question of whether it is irrational that 'our society is not marked by participatory processes of decision making'[54] and the question of whether 'action research' provides a way of distinguishing ideas that are more systematically distorted by ideology from those that are less systematically distorted?[55]

The constitution of an 'action research' community presupposes the superiority of a particular form of rationality based on the idea that minimum ideological distortion is achieved in the 'ideal speech situation'. Yet it cannot be uncritically assumed that a community of 'action researchers' operating within a legal and administrative framework that is allegedly 'irrational' is going to be any more successful in approaching the 'ideal speech situation' than any other community that is interested in education. Therefore, I believe that Carr and Kemmis make a mistake when they go on to recommend a form of teacher professionalism in which teachers alone are supposed to be able to make informed educational judgments:

> in these times of increasing bureaucratic management in educa-
> tion, the profession must organise itself to support and protect
> its professionalism.[56]

As I argued in Chapter 1, the professionalization of educational theory is supportive of, and in the 1960s led to the entrenchment of, the very conception of rationality that Carr and Kemmis reject. We may wonder whether the effect of professionalizing educational practice within an administrative framework that still reflects an objectivistic conception of rationality would not further entrench that conception of rationality. In other words, we may wonder whether teachers are in any better position to make informed educational judgments free from prejudice and outside interference than 'professional educational theorists' employed in the colleges and departments of education. Putting it more strongly, we may wonder whether Carr and Kemmis's proposal would lead to the so-called 'professional judgment' of teachers becoming simply another device for theoretically legitimizing an objectivistic conception of rationality.

For me, the notions of 'professionalism' and 'practical discursive rationality' are logically incompatible. Educational decision-making cannot be both the open process presupposed in the notion of an 'ideal speech situation' and the closed process presupposed in the notion of professionalism. If teachers were to organize themselves in the ways that Carr and Kemmis recommend, then it is not clear from what perspective or even from what source the knowledge, skills and abilities requisite for action research would be supplied in order that teachers might become action researchers. It is also unclear how a reconciliation would be achieved between the need to exclude so-called 'outsiders', who might distort teacher discourse and the need for educational institutions to allow their members to participate in the wider social practices of communication, decision-making and collaborative action[57] that is required by Carr and Kemmis's appropriation of Habermas's prescription for a rational society.[58] This is the fundamental problem for Carr and Kemmis: they fail to show how the professionalization of educational practice is compatible with practical discursive rationality and hence they fail to grasp the key question as to how educational theory might serve to mediate between the various interests that compete, in order that we should be able to decide what to do in educational institutions.

Notes and References

1   HEIDEGGER, M. (1962) *Being and Time*, p. 194.
2   *Ibid.*
3   TAYLOR, C. (1985) *Philosophical Papers*, vol. 2, p. 17.
4   HEIDEGGER, M., 1962, pp. 194–5.
5   I refer to the report by Professor Martin Gardener of Southampton University that was published in the *British Medical Journal* on 16 February 1990. See also *The Times* on that day for a description of the events that surrounded the publication.
6   cf. SCHLEIERMACHER, F. (Ed.) (1977) *Hermeneutics: the Handwritten Manuscripts*, Kimmerle H. Scholars Press, Missoula, Montana.
7   cf. DILTHEY, W. (Ed.) (1976) *Selected Writings*, Rickman H.P. Cambridge.
8   GADAMER, H.G. (1975a) *Truth and Method*, p. 240.
9   LINGE, H.E. (1976) 'Introduction' to GADAMER, H.G., *Philosophical Hermeneutics*, p. xv.

10 GADAMER, H.G., 1975a, p. 273.

11 WARNOCK, M. (1979) *Education: A Way Ahead*, ch. 2.

12 For a further development of this idea see the work of L.A. REID, especially his *Meaning and the Arts*, 1969, Allen and Unwin, and more recently his *Ways of Understanding and Education*, 1986, Heinemann. See also GREGER, S. (1972) 'Aesthetic Meaning', *Journal of Philosophy of Education* 6,2.

13 GADAMER, H.G., 1975a, p. 347.

14 *Ibid.*, p. 248.

15 See GARFINKEL, A. (1981) *Forms of Explanation*, for a development of this point.

16 I gather that such promotion procedures are becoming increasingly popular within industrial organizations. However, I am not aware of any formally recognized procedures of this type within educational organizations.

17 See, for example, the letters column of the *Glasgow Herald* immediately following the publication of the 'Main Report' referred to in Chapter 2.

18 GADAMER, H.G. (1981) *Reason in the Age of Science*, p. 89.

19 *Ibid.*, p. 109.

20 GADAMER, H.G. (1975b) 'Hermeneutics and social science', p. 316.

21 RORTY, R. (1980) *Philosophy and the Mirror of Nature*, pp. 385–6. Notice that Rorty departs from Gadamer's position when he writes: 'it is the commonplace fact that people may develop doubts about what they are doing, and thereupon begin to discourse in ways *incommensurable* with those they used previously' (my emphasis). By using the term 'incommensurable', Rorty seems to me to fall into Kuhn's earlier difficulty of attempting to reconcile the ideas of 'theory-preference' and 'revolutionary conceptual shifts'. If Rorty were to accept Kuhn's later resolution of this difficulty and adopt the idea of epistemology as communally agreed interpretation, his account of abnormal discourse might be more plausible than one which seems to suggest that abnormal discourse floats free of any communally agreed norms.

22 WITTGENSTEIN, L. (1977) *Culture and Value*, p. 27.

23 The term 'critical theory' is usually used to describe the work of a group of German philosophers known as the 'Frankfurt School'. This group includes Horkheimer, Adorno, Marcuse and Habermas. These philosophers may be considered to be interested mainly in the work of Marx and Freud.

24 See the Bibliography for some of Habermas's publications. For a more complete list see MCCARTHY, T. (1978) *The Critical Theory of Jurgen Habermas*, pp. 443–64.

25 A reader who is new to the idea of a critical theory may like to consult GEUSS, R. (1981) *The Idea of a Critical Theory*. Alternatively, BERNSTEIN, R.J. (1976) *The Restructuring of Social and Political Theory*. For a more detailed account of the work of Habermas, see MCCARTHY, T., 1978.

26 HABERMAS, J. (1977) 'A review of Gadamer's truth and method', p. 360.

27 See HABERMAS, J. (1975) 'On systematically distorted communication'.

28 HABERMAS, J. (1972) *Knowledge and Human Interests*.

29 In a recent collection titled *Habermas and Modernity*, 1985, the editor R.J.

BERNSTEIN describes Habermas as a defender of 'the legacy of western rationality' (p. 25) and in the same volume GIDDENS writes of Habermas's preoccupation with isolating the conditions of rational decision making' (p. 95). These writers support the view that Habermas's work is an attempt to produce a objectivistic theory of rationality.

30 GADAMER, H.G. (1976) *Philosophical Hermeneutics*, pp. 18–43.
31 GADAMER, H.G. (1970) 'Replik'.
32 GADAMER, H.G., 1970, pp. 315–6.
33 GADAMER, H.G., 1976, p. 42.
34 HABERMAS, J. (1984) *The Theory of Communicative Action*.
35 HABERMAS, J. (1973) A 'Postscript' to *Knowledge and Human Interests*, p. 168.
36 HABERMAS, J. (1970) 'Towards a theory of communicative competence', p. 143.
37 HABERMAS, J. (1976) *Legitimation Crisis*, p. 113.
38 HESSE, M. (1980) *Revolutions and Reconstructions in the Philosophy of Science* p. 219.
39 HESSE, M., 1980, p. 225.
40 Quoted in McCARTHY, T. (1973) 'A theory of communicative competence', *Philosophy of the Social Sciences*, iii, p. 140.
41 As has been pointed out, educational researchers have not been insensitive to the 'protest against the scientific detachment of traditional psychological and psychometric studies', for example, NISBET, J. (1980) 'Educational research: The state of the art', in DOCKRELL, W. and HAMILTON, D. (Eds) (1980) *Rethinking Educational Research*, p. 6. Nor have researchers been unaware of the difficulty of becoming a full participant in a community being researched when their introduction into and departure from that community are planned in advance and particularly when the intention behind their involvement is unconnected with the common concerns of the community.
42 CARR, W. and KEMMIS, S. (1983) *Becoming Critical: Knowing through Action Research*.
43 See also GRUNDY, S. (1987) *Curriculum: Product or Praxis*.
44 CARR, W. and KEMMIS, S., 1983, p. 118.
45 cf. BROCK-UTNE, B. (1980) 'What is educational action research?' *CARN Bulletin* no. 4, p. 10.
46 CARR, W. and KEMMIS, S., 1983, p. 173.
47 *Ibid.*, p. 179.
48 *Ibid.*, p. 182.
49 *Ibid.*, p. 184.
50 *Ibid.*, p. 145.
51 *Ibid.*
52 *Ibid.*, p. 161.
53 *Ibid.*, p. 184.
54 *Ibid.*, p. 181.
55 *Ibid.*, p. 177.
56 *Ibid.*, p. 198.
57 *Ibid.*, p. 192.
58 HABERMAS, J. (1971) *Towards a Rational Society*.

Chapter 6

A Philosophical Alternative

The move away from objectivism and the set of educational implications that coheres with it has led us to develop a hermeneutic conception of rationality that has implications for teaching, theorizing, curriculum and management. In this final chapter I explain these implications in greater detail and argue that institutional changes are necessary for us to move towards the realization of these alternatives and to challenge the dominance of objectivism within education. First, let me try to bring the various arguments that have been presented in the previous three chapters together and to outline the general thrust of my philosophical alternative to objectivism that is based on Kuhn's account of natural science.

In Chapter 3, we saw that educational theory might be viewed as a subset of an overall network of theory that develops scientifically. In Chapter 4, we saw that natural scientific and other types of theory development were parasitic upon each other because of the 'linguistic division of labour' both across communities of theorists and between communities of theorists. We saw also that theory-preference is always under-determined by observational data and that values guide the choices that theorists make. However, those choices are not made on the basis of a list of criteria that a community simply applies. Instead, choices are made on the basis of interpretations within some commonly agreed temporary framework that binds the community together. In Chapter 5, we saw that these interpretations involve both theoretical and practical reorientation and that the distinction between practical and theoretical interest is more one of degree rather than kind. We also considered how Habermas's notion of 'the ideal speech situation' might be both an important interest which guides our interpretations and a notion that helps us to avoid the idea that educational theory can only be a response to immediate practical problems.

Finally, we examined the limitations of 'action research' as a strategy for change in education.

We may respond to these limitations by suggesting that even though theory and practice are coextensive and everybody is, to a different extent, both theoretically and practically inclined, that is no reason to doubt that there might be some advantage to be gained in instituting what might be called a theoretical endeavour, that attempts to reinterpret what was going on across a range of other endeavours, in the hope that such a reinterpretation might make for a greater perspicuity in the choices that face us. The distinction between experimental and theoretical natural scientists may form a model here: just as the theoretical physicist cannot proceed for long without reference to the work of the experimentalist, so too we may suggest that educational development would be enhanced if there was an 'essential tension' between work of immediate practical relevance to schools and colleges and 'theoretical work' that is not of obvious practical relevance but that nevertheless enables us critically to evaluate our established practice. By constantly interpreting what each other is doing, teachers and 'theorists' may avoid a loss of meaning of those terms that are of central importance to the evaluation of rival interpretations. On this view our ordinary idea of a conversation serves as a guide to the importance of sustaining a conversation between those whose interest is predominantly 'within an endeavour' and those whose interest is predominantly 'across a range of endeavours' constituting educational institutions and their typical forms of discourse.

However, we should not make the mistake of imagining that theorists should look for revolutionary change in education as might be suggested in Kuhn's earlier work. Instead, we might suggest that there should be an 'essential tension'[1] between innovation and tradition in educational theory and practice and between institutions in which rival conceptions of rationality dominate. In my view, we may make progress when we place all aspects of education in jeopardy though not at the same time. Hence no set of ideas or practices should dominate completely and we should argue for our particular points of view accordingly. In that way there is also an essential tension between normal and abnormal discourse so that normal discourse may form a touchstone against which progress is judged. For example, like Kuhn we might denigrate the idea that 'divergent thinking'[2] is more important than 'convergent thinking' in research. We may make the practical point that a theorist who questioned every anomalous observation simply would never complete a first research project and that tradition gives stability to the evaluation of innovatory proposals.

Also, just as Kuhn recognizes the role that experiment plays in scientific research by providing 'anchoring points' on which to pin a developing network of theory, at least temporarily, we may note that demonstrable practical success in education also provides 'anchoring points' on which to support our arguments for change.

Therefore, we should place greater emphasis on tradition in educational theory and practice. We may resist some innovatory curricular and managerial initiatives on the grounds that we do not have a stable tradition of educational discourse against which to evaluate such innovations. Even though there may be considerable political pressure on educational theorists to innovate, we might be on firm ground in resisting this pressure and paying far more attention to achieving a consensus between educational theorist and teacher regarding those innovations that command widespread support. This suggestion would involve changes in the way in which educational theory is presently conceived in relation to policy-making and implementation. Policy-making would need to be more open than it is at present.

In order to explain this point we may compare private and state sector schooling. Many parents prefer to send their children to private schools. It might be suggested that this is because private schools are better resourced, have pupils whose parents are generally more articulate than their state counterparts and so on. However, it can also be suggested that private schools are characterized by a stability not present in the state sector. The private school seems not to have to respond to anything like the rate of curricular change that has recently faced and currently faces the state sector. It can be argued that the private school curriculum is basically academic and that changes like those towards computing or craft, design and technology can be planned against a fairly settled curricular background. In other words, those who work in the private sector have a more settled form of practical discourse which enables them to appraise educational developments. This option is not open to the state sector, which takes the brunt of the forward thrust of foundationalist empiricism, not cushioned by any financial reserve and more immediately compelled to accept and implement those recent curricular developments that have been largely directed towards the less able child.

The private sector has some less able children too, however, and it might be suggested that parts of the state sector might emulate the private sector by deciding simply not to accept uncritically many of the new 'exciting curricular developments' and instead adapt, update and modify many of the old.[3] The empiricist's idea that learning involves the accumulation of relevant bits of knowledge might be rejected in favour of a hermeneutic idea of learning which stresses the importance of moving from present 'prejudice' towards future under-standing. In other words, the emphasis might be shifted away from a narrow vocationalism back towards an ideal of more liberal education within the state sector, the detailed content of which might only be important to the extent that it enables learners to go on and find things out for themselves — and encourages them to do so. In this way, the manner in which teachers view what they are doing and the satisfaction that they get from their job become crucial determinants of the success of their teaching.

Finally, we might find it profitable to cease regarding education as a sort of technology that can be instituted and/or deployed to solve any social problem we face. I have already criticized the idea of an exclusively vocational education as if, for instance, education could resolve the problem of unemployment. A similar criticism may be advanced against the idea of an exclusively political education for democratic autonomy. As Edgley comments:

> political education for autonomy raises the question: should schools train revolutionaries? The very idea is [a] fantasy ...
> Its being so indicates the strict limits of education's political power, and of its powers in political education.[4]

The point is that education is simply one factor in the development of a society and is a facilitator of just one conversation among the many that people engage in during the course of their lives. We should not imagine that by setting educational objectives from without the edu-cational community our social problems will necessarily decrease, as if educational theory were some kind of applied science. Instead, we should note that pure research in the natural sciences has had far greater technological 'pay-off' than any attempt to tailor research to satisfy some perceived need; for this reason perhaps educational theorists should emulate the natural scientific community by seeking and claiming much greater say in the selection of their educational research problems.

Curriculum

We have seen how the idea of a network of theories and practices is a powerful device for explaining both the rationality of individuals and of communities. Now if it is accepted that one of the things that education should do is to promote rationality then it looks as if teaching might be viewed as an endeavour that enables students to develop their own linguistic networks in a coherent way. It looks too as if this view has implications for curriculum: the search for overall coherence is likely to be enhanced if learners have the opportunity to extend their horizons on the basis of a wide range of conversations with the bearers of the prejudice of tradition. This means that educational institutions should be organized so that a wide area of the network that a society currently accepts as the embodiment of its ethical norms, its best theories and its most useful practices, should be presented to learners.

When we describe forms of knowledge, crafts, practices or curricular subjects, we refer to rough areas of this network that include both theories and practices. Some readers may be concerned that I still use these two terms as if a clear distinction could be drawn between them. I should explain that I use them simply because they are established and because they draw attention to two important emphases: first, that some human interests are more immediate and obvious than others; second, that some human endeavours seem to depend less on the use of words than others. For example, joinery might be imagined to consist in rather more actions than words and biology might be imagined to consist of rather more words than actions. Cooking might be imagined to be of more immediate interest than hermeneutics and to consist in rather fewer words and so on. For me, it does not matter how our network of what we might call endeavours is divided up, nor what its constituents are called — the important consideration is that boundaries between constituents can never be sharply drawn nor can they be justified in logic.

All this makes policy-making and educational planning very difficult if not impossible for objectivists. It is not even as if an elaborate diagram could be drawn showing connections and overlapping subsets of currently established subjects, vocational preparations, communities of practitioners, endeavours or whatever we might like to call the curricular constituents. Even if a multi-dimensional model could be constructed to represent the fibres in a curricular network, the complexity of that model and the rate at which it would need to be revised, is likely to render it useless to those administrators charged with the responsibility of getting appropriate people in appropriate rooms at appropriate times for the purpose of education.

This lack of precision does not mean that educational policy-making and administration are impossible nor that blurred curricular boundaries are useless. It does mean though that we need to change our way of doing things so that we do not invest much effort in the pursuit of an impossible and for me ultimately incoherent goal of objectifying the curriculum. Instead, we may recognize that at any time we have a variety of people competent in various parts of our network of endeavours and we arrange for some of these people to be in particular places at particular times so that opportunities might be provided for others to maximize both their own and everyone else's coherence by assimilating and challenging the prejudices of tradition.

I expect that this proposal would involve both full-time teachers providing a core coverage of the curricular network and peripatetic teachers who might broaden that core for some students and who might provide points of entry to parts of the network for other students. As many teachers are aware, some students find that the practical leads into the theoretical. These students are unlikely to be intrigued by definitions and abstract principles. Instead, they might begin by examining applications with which they are familiar, moving on to look for explanations of why things are the way that they are, how they came to be that way and what developments are likely to take place in the future.

While I accept that there will always be important arguments about whether a person with a particular specialist background should be employed as a teacher, I do not believe that we can develop precise guidelines to govern such selection. It may be that the vast amount of effort that is currently being expended in implementing a 'common curriculum' in England and Wales[5] is misplaced for, in many ways, there always was a common curriculum in these countries. There were variations between schools and undoubtedly there were some deficiencies, yet it is not at all clear that future curricular provision is going to be much more uniform, particularly when it is reported that there is a serious shortage of certain specialist teachers. It may be that a lot of this effort is going into the documentation of the ways in which a particular apportionment of time matches a supposedly precise description of what the British Government believe to be a 'broad and balanced' curriculum. We might do better to concentrate on improving the quality of teaching and the quality of the arguments that administrators might use to support particular educational decisions in the context in which those decisions are actually made.

For me, the particular configuration of teaching specialisms that are provided at any one time is not so important as the quality of the teaching that takes place, for it is teachers who encourage students to have the confidence to extend their horizons. It may be that those teachers who have wide experience are in a better position to give this confidence and encouragement than those whose experience is limited. It may, therefore, be worth instituting some sort of exchange arrangements whereby different sorts of worker, which includes teachers, exchange roles from time to time so that the peripatetic support that I mentioned earlier could be provided readily and so that teachers themselves might extend their own range of interests. In addition, this proposal may lead to an improvement in the status of teaching as more people become aware of the nature of the work that teachers do. In turn, this improvement may make teaching more attractive as a career thus helping governments to avoid having to pay some teachers more than others on the basis of their specialism. Such market rigour may hinder the development of cooperation and mutual respect within educational institutions.

My account of curriculum supports the idea of continuing education for I do not prescribe set routes through a curricular network for set ages of people. Instead, people are encouraged to work their own way through the network as and when they are interested. Someone might notice that all this flexibility sits uncomfortably close to the objectivistic modular curriculum that I criticized in Chapter 2. However, for me the only objectivism that need concern us is the undoubted demand for some form of certification of learning that is clearly understandable and reasonably valid. I agree with M. Warnock that some form of graded tests may be the most appropriate way of meeting this demand.[6] However, such certification need not lead us to try to objectify all other aspects of education, nor need we let it dominate to the extent that every learning outcome is formally assessed.[7] Grading loses its point if it is unreliable or if it is too difficult to understand. No one is fooled by the attempt to suggest that it is possible finely to discriminate between human performances, nor are they much interested in perusing a lengthy profile that attempts to certify that level of discrimination.

Teaching

Recently much has been made both of the idea of a practice generally[8] and of the particular idea that teaching is a practice.[9] It has been imagined that by stressing the idea of practitioners formulating and developing their own policy and recognizing their own internal goods or standards of excellence that somehow some of the deforming aspects of institutional objectivism can be avoided. This emphasis is rather like Gadamer's attempt to reinstate the notion of *praxis* and is closely related to the action research movement that I described in the previous chapter. We noted that the idea of a community of action researchers developing their own internal standards of linguistic procedure is not only undesirable but also impossible. A certain amount of romanticism seems to fuel these movements — it is as if life would be so much better if we were to form sort of craft-guilds on islands immune from external influences.

In order to avoid these romantic overtones, I choose to refer to a network of endeavours into which students might be inducted rather than a network of practices. Let us note as a rough generalization that this induction is often best achieved by moving from interest within an endeavour to interest across a range of endeavours. We have already seen how terms in one form of discourse are commensurable with the use of those terms in another and we have begun to consider endeavours as overlapping subsets of activities and thoughts which are supported by people whose interests and forms of discourse also overlap. This degree of overlap is essential to my account of teaching for in trying to get someone to understand an endeavour I need to draw upon a common language and a common background of shared experiences and shared conceptions of what is worth valuing. Unless my conversational partner has already participated in the endeavour, in which case she already has some understanding of it, then there has to be some entering wedge by means of which we can develop a shared understanding and so get a purchase on the endeavour. Our common experiences and interests provide this entering wedge.

The idea of inducting someone into a practice that is self-contained leads both to the idea that all aspects of practices remain closed to the possibility of understanding on the part of those 'on the outside', and to the idea that understanding a practice involves a sort of conversion which occurs all at once.

Both ideas are untenable. I do not wish to argue that when someone 'grasps an idea', 'gets my meaning' or 'cottons on', as it were, something like a conversion does not appear to have taken place; rather I suggest that such conversions occur throughout an explanation. That is not to suggest that such conversions always involve some sort of activity whereby the learner 'tries something out for herself'. Instead, such conversions often involve nothing more than the learner identifying a 'family resemblance' between the two uses of a term, with one of which the learner is familiar and the other of which the learner is trying to understand.

When people are interested in a particular endeavour, then they may simply watch and interpret the endeavour on the basis of their own 'horizon of expectations'. Alternatively they may actually work with a group as apprentices. Learning may also take place when an inexperienced teacher presents the prejudices of tradition simply by telling students about an endeavour. However, many experienced teachers seem to recognize that learning, interpreting and understanding converge when they interpret an endeavour for the learner on the basis of their having an understanding of the way that that endeavour relates to other endeavours. People's understanding may be enhanced when their 'horizon of expectation' is fused with the prejudices of tradition that stores the interpretive work of people's previous attempts to understand. The teacher takes on the role of conversational partner and the learner's useless 'prejudices' are discarded as a result of the recognition that the teacher's prejudice is superior in the added dimensions of ability and insight it confers; that is to say, that 'prejudices' are discarded as a result of the recognition of another viewpoint's superior 'authority'. To recognize that authority is to take the first step towards being taught.

While the recognition of authority enables students to learn it does not determine their learning. The experienced teacher is not just presenting the prejudices of tradition in the form of a structured series of texts designed to increase students' knowledge on the basis of maxims like 'move from the known to the unknown' or analogies and metaphors. The teacher is also trying to intrigue students into posing new questions for themselves, and then to see that the answers to these questions pose new questions and so on, in the hope that students will be able to go on on their own. As Gadamer puts it, greater understanding may lead to 'a growth in inner awareness of future possibilities'[10] which in turn intrigues the learner into reinterpreting what presently goes on in order to try to resolve a tension between 'future possibilities' and present understanding.

Educational Theory

This account of teaching as a species of 'conversation' may also serve as an account of educational theory. Just as teaching, on my argument, involves the presentation of the prejudices of tradition in order to enable learners to maximize the overall coherence of their network of endeavours, so too educational theory might be supposed to involve the presentation of the prejudices of tradition in the form of a coherent narrative with which to engage people in 'the conversation of mankind',[11] to use Oakeshott's phrase. Oakeshott speaks thus to draw attention to the way in which tension between 'present condition' and 'future possibilities' is never finally resolved but serves as an impetus for a continuing conversation between a variety of forms of discourse, all of which are concerned, in one way or another, critically to reappraise various features of the human predicament.

On this view there is no distinction to be made between a narrative and dialogue. The use of the phrase 'coherent narrative' is not meant to imply that there is any definitive narrative to be produced. Instead, it is to suggest that to tell a story about what is going on is just as likely to intrigue people into reinterpreting their predicament as any other form of discourse in which people might engage. The analogy between educational theory and teaching is not total, however: the teacher-student relationship involves an asymmetry in authority relations not necessarily present in the case of educational theory. If a student fails to understand, because the teacher is unable to engage the student in conversation, the teacher-student relationship as regards its pedagogic intent breaks down. In such cases teachers may attempt to change their orientation by attempting to get students to learn something else or the same thing in a different way. However, their status as teachers depends upon their ability to engage most students in conversation for most of the time; hence the onus is on the student to attempt to understand something of other endeavours in order to further a conversation with a teacher. Teachers are 'in authority' because they are acknowledged to be an authority for most of the time. In other words, they are assumed to be bearers of a tradition for the purpose of encouraging and enabling others to join that tradition.

By contrast, the educational theorist carries no such status. It is a contingent matter whether educational theory engages a person's interest. In the case of other people's failure to understand or respond, the theorist may simply give up for the time being. However, there is no easy equivalent in educational theory of 'waiting for the student to understand'. Nor is there any reason why people should attempt to understand other endeavours — they may simply deny that educational theory has any relevance to their lives and choose to solve their problems pragmatically. This may well be a suitable response. It seems to me that for educational theory to have any point, it must show people how things might look if they understood and responded to it. Moreover, it must convince people that the possible state of affairs it adumbrates is desirable and achievable. In other words, without some idea of the ways in which people might improve their present predicament, it is not clear how the educational theorist could ever present a convincing narrative.[12]

I do not wish to suggest that every theory should contain practical recommendations. Nor do I wish to suggest that theorizing cannot include changing one's practical orientation through conversation with others.[13] For example, within endeavours, simply talking about what to do next is theorizing in a very important sense. However, people are also interested in the way that many endeavours might cohere and give sense to the way that they frame their lives as a whole. That is to say, no one is exclusively theoretical or practical or exclusively a parent, a bricklayer or a teacher. Instead, people's interests extend outward from all their practical involvements towards a search for this coherence. As a result, educated people continue to reformulate what J.P. White has called a 'life plan'[14] throughout their lives. Such a 'plan' has many of the characteristics of a theoretic network — it involves assumptions, claims and predictions that may be modified and, just as a theoretic network is rearranged to incorporate new evidence, so too a 'life plan' is modified in the light of changing circumstances. Such changing circumstances prompt people to look again at their 'life plans' and to reflect upon whether the replacement of one part of those plans might lead to greater coherence within the reformulated whole.

This principle of maximizing the coherence of a network of endeavours governs both the way that individuals learn and the way that a society develops. Since people are members of society, it is hardly surprising that my accounts of educational theory and teaching are similar. It should be noted, however, that in a sense I refer to two different networks when I discuss teaching and educational theory — one network relates to the individual and the other to a group or society. In many cases these networks coincide and in other cases they differ. As the notion of coherence cannot be made objectively precise, there will always be a variety of ways that an individual or a group could maximize the overall coherence of either network. While it should not be imagined that it makes sense to consider whether a particular action or idea maximizes overall coherence, let alone whether such maximization could be determined, the differences between peoples' networks coupled with the extent of the agreement between them makes it possible to discuss whether someone has learnt and whether a society has progressed over a period of time.

We should note, too, that both individuals and groups go through periods of crisis during which complete sets of ideas and practices are rejected. It is easy to find examples of these crises both when individuals adjust after some traumatic event and when groups come to find it unacceptable to smoke in public, to own certain breeds of dog, to beat children in school or to be governed by a dictator. In the last case and sometimes in the former cases the crisis is terrifying. It may be that by placing the notion of an ideal consensus more firmly within the set of values that guides the choices we make and by ceasing to elevate any particular theory or set of theories above all others that some of this trauma and terror could be avoided.

The objectivist's attempt to elevate a set of ideas and practices above others may only serve to heighten the tension between individual and societal networks. People may only be prepared to give up something of their freedom to choose at work if they believe that this loss is more than balanced by a gain in material well-being and freedom at home. If doubts develop about this balance then tension increases between endeavours at work and endeavours at home. This latter point forms the basis of a 'horizon of expectation' that goes beyond a concern with material well-being and aspires towards endeavours in which non-coercive human relationships flourish. An objectivistic conception of rationality places these endeavours 'at the margin' of the societal network by embodying both the idea that human relationships should be treated as means rather than as ends in themselves and the further idea that in undertaking our administrative tasks we are not morally implicated.

Therefore, the promotion of a crude form of vocationalism may give rise to a further tension between the endeavour to educate and other endeavours into which students are supposed to be initiated. The idea that students should continue to form 'horizons of expectation' that intrigue them into posing ever new questions concerning the possibility of understanding what is going on around them, may conflict with the idea that students should be prepared for a 'world of work' that depends for its effective operation upon workers severely limiting their 'horizons of expectation' to a reality that is defined for them and is to be uncritically accepted. For example, rather than the assumption that many students might be demotivated because the curriculum is alleged to be insufficiently relevant to the 'world of work', such lack of motivation might be explained on the grounds of a student's perception of the quality of the experience that work is supposed to offer.

Alternatively, the notion of education as initiation[15] may be thought by some to be impossible, irrelevant or effete, when the structures into which students are supposed to be initiated are themselves fragmented by a loss of common meaning and values that some writers[16] allege has taken place. Moreover, in some cases there may be a tension between a sense of the loss of community, identity and values outside a school, and a strong sense of community within. Hence it may be that students are demotivated not so much by the quality of their experiences within the school but more by the prospect of the soured outside or lack of any sense of community that awaits them in the 'real' world. School may be seen to fail to prepare people for work, not so much because of an inappropriate curriculum but more because the sense of community generated or not in a wider society seems unreal to a student population led to believe that reality is a cohesive notion defined *inter alia* by the importance attached to 'the world of work' and the unquestioning assumptions attaching to it and to them.

To take another example, the recent industrial action taken by teachers may be explained as a protest against what they see as the diminution of their role to that of a technician responding to educational needs that are determined in abstraction from their influence. As a result, the quality of teaching deteriorates to the extent that it becomes dominated by 'external goods'. The set of meanings that once sustained a predominance of 'internal goods' within teaching is now so diminished that teachers take industrial action in pursuit of more 'external goods' as might befit any group of workers whose objectives are largely set 'externally' and that is led to believe that it should be rewarded according to its success in achieving those objectives. The idea that the constant attempt to replace 'internal goods' with 'external goods' might lead to a loss of a common sense of identity and/or purpose within an endeavour is something with which empiricism is unable to deal. Within empiricism, debate about common purpose and commitment is taken as an indication of weakness, because such debate implies that the participants have an interest in their endeavours that might prejudice their work as morally-neutral technicians. Whereas, according to my thesis, such a debate is an indication of the strength of an endeavour.

Teachers may be increasingly suspicious both of those attempts to set pay scales on the basis that extrinsic motivation is all that is important, and those attempts to find the one form of discourse, like computing, marketing or management, that is going to act as a determinant for the legitimacy and value of all others and that is going to provide them with a new sort of theory to inform future practice. Instead, many teachers may come to accept that teaching is an endeavour that sustains its own values and shared commitments into which trainee teachers might be inducted by a sort of apprenticeship system, and which has as its central point of identity and its prime common meaning that the point of learning is to be able to 'go on on one's own', that is, to be able to modify one's epistemological prejudices by continually reinterpreting one's perception of one's predicament in all the various forms that that reinterpretation might take.

The Validation of Educational Theory

It may appear as if educational theorists are interpreters who present narratives that attempt to engage us in a similar way to the narratives that are produced by poets and novelists. Indeed, it might be claimed that many poets and novelists engage our interest rather more than some educational theorists! However, I want to argue that educational theory can be validated in a way that is not necessarily open to other interpreters. It seems to me that there is little point in having an account of theory unless that account includes a way of validating theories. My account of educational theory as an interpretive endeavour points towards the idea that an 'ideal consensus' may serve as a 'regulative ideal' to guide theory-preference. But, as we noted earlier, this idea is based on an 'ungrounded hope' rather than an 'objective criterion' and even though objectivists may be deluded in their belief that such a criterion can be formulated and usefully applied, their present dominance within educational policy-making institutions is likely to militate against any institutional changes that might be proposed as part of an educational theory that is regarded as validated on the basis of an 'ungrounded hope'.

Of course all endeavours contain their own ways of validating theories, based on the 'internal goods' that people value such as style, coherence and authenticity in discourse. 'Internal goods', however, are continually being transmuted within an endeavour and there remains the problem of differentiating between such transmutation and the deformation that occurs when 'external goods' such as power, status and money start to dominate the endeavour. In other words, the common view of what constitutes style, authenticity and so on changes and it is not necessarily apparent whether such change has been brought about by an undesirable deformation of the endeavour or a desirable and normal change in the meaning that these terms have for the people who support the endeavour. The writers mentioned in the introduction argue that empiricist epistemology is necessarily distorting and they invoke the notions of 'authentic community' and 'communal solidarity'[17] in order to suggest that the members of a community know when their endeavour is so severely deformed that relationships within the community become distortive and sometimes even exploitative. Authenticity is supposed, by these writers, to be achieved when the members of a community reflect upon their immediate self-interests and distinguish between those interests that are distorted by ideology and those that are not. In this way, immediate self-interests are transcended by the reflective-discursive process so that people may identify their 'real' interests and act in 'solidarity' with one another.

This transcendence may take place but it is hardly likely to satisfy the objectivist who will expect educational theory to go beyond a mere recital of the ways of validating theories internally. We may make two responses to the objectivist here. We can either suppose that there is an unbridgeable gulf between objectivist and hermeneuticist and go on appealing to notions of 'communal solidarity' and so on in the hope that objectivists will see the folly of their ways. Alternatively, we can grant to the objectivist that there is a need to go beyond the internal validation of educational theory without our assuming that there is some sort of social reality that can serve as an external 'touchstone': we can suggest that it is the forms of 'normal' discourse that happen to enmesh with objectivistic and hermeneutic theories that provide the 'touchstone' for their comparison.

We get no further towards validating educational theories against each other if we continue to view theory or practice as things that can be measured, rather like weighing apples or assessing happiness or whatever. Nor do we get any further towards such validation if we continue to present educational theories as visions of a moral/political nirvana in which all problems of theory validation disappear in some version of a communal 'wonderland'. Even if practical discourse were as deformed by instrumentalism, as writers like MacIntyre, Taylor and Gadamer suggest, we should only be able to reorient our values and reject instrumentalism if we accepted that the ideas embodied in the term 'communal solidarity' could function as regulative ideals to guide the development of educational theory. Such theory would need to have internal standards of validation that could be invoked to appraise all related social endeavours and these endeavours would need to be continually discursively validated by an on-going fundamental critique.

The problem with theories of this kind that present a moral-political vision, which, if realized, would end all problems of theory validation, is that they tend to be catch-all theories that cannot themselves be validated and certainly not by their own criteria. Any predictions made within such theories are always subject to the proviso that we do not yet have anything approaching 'communal solidarity'. Instead, the attempt to achieve a moral-political vision involves starting from objectivistic theories that presently inform our endeavours such as the theories that I discussed in Chapter 2. That means comparing present endeavours against alternatives that would reflect to a greater extent the notions of 'democratic participation' and 'communal solidarity'. We might expect our educational theories to guide the setting up of alternative institutional structures within which such alternative endeavours might flourish. I do not mean that every educational theory should involve some proposals for alternative institutional practices but that the search for such proposals should function for the theorist like the search for abnormal discourse — that is, as a guide to practice that is occasionally realized.

My argument is that at present many of our institutional practices in education are sustained by theories that are firmly rooted in objectivism. I am attempting to argue for alternative and better institutional practices that are rooted in a hermeneutic conception of educational theory. However, I believe that its internal standards are insufficient to validate that attempt and that I still need to appeal to some 'touchstone' that will provide us with the means to validate theories against one another. I suggest that we can make little progress towards achieving a realization of the notions of 'communal solidarity' and 'democratic participation' unless we make practical changes that lead to institutions with different managerial structures flourishing alongside each other. The 'touchstone' by which these institutions could then be compared would doubtless be similar to the forms of 'normal' discourse that are presently used to appraise those institutions that embody objectivism. However, this modest bow in the direction of objectivism is necessary to enable us to make some kind of theoretic comparisons. Practical changes should be set in train and become established so that future theoretical progress may be made.[18]

Educational theory may remain ossified in objectivism unless institutional changes are made that reflect alternative conceptions of rationality. In other words, however many convincing narratives are produced extolling the virtues of a practical-discursive conception of rationality, theoretical progress is unlikely to be made unless some institutions are changed so that they embody such a conception of rationality. I suggest that the validation of hermeneutic social theories depends upon subjecting the claims of rival hermeneutic and objectivistic theories to the court of appeal that is constituted in and exhibited by the ways that endeavours are both alleged to be and actually are changed by them and that implies institutional changes also. To this suggestion it might be objected that the possibility of any radical conceptual innovation rules out procedures involving prediction. However, I am not proposing that statements be tested against the future: I am proposing that endeavours that project their own tradition into the future can be compared with one another. In effect, I propose that the problem of conceptual innovation, that renders traditional empirical social theory implausible, may be partly overcome by comparing endeavours, which necessarily involve their own conceptual innovations. My equivalent to Lakatos's idea of a 'research programme'[19] is the idea of an institutional endeavour such as that of a college. Just as Lakatos urges us not to judge theories individually but as a series that emanates from a decision to treat some theories as unproblematic while others are under test, so I urge the value of seeking to validate educational theory by making the legal changes necessary for groups of endeavours such as colleges and schools to be set up in ways that reflect a concern with practical discursive rationality. These endeavours may then be compared with their objectivistic counterparts.

On this view, institutional endeavours are allowed to flourish alongside one another. However, if we are to avoid the kind of relativism that Feyerabend advocates, it may be necessary to agree both upon some time scale within which rival endeavours are to be compared and those forms of 'normal' discourse that are to serve as 'touchstones' for this comparison. Objectivists would certainly require this much. They would insist that educational theories informed by hermeneutics include a statement indicating those conditions under which they could be falsified. In order to get theoretical comparison going and place objectivism in jeopardy, it seems to me that hermeneuticists must acquiesce in this requirement. However, their acquiescence enables them to have some basis for hoping that objectivists themselves might adjust their endeavours on the basis of the conversations that they have with hermeneuticists. In other words, there remains the hope that by a process of gradual holistic adjustment, hermeneutics might come to challenge objectivism as the dominant social theory within which our institutional, managerial and validatory requirements are conceived.

I propose the setting-up of some educational institutions staffed by those who are sympathetic to the idea of practical discursive rationality to rival existing educational institutions that embody the idea of hierarchical managerialism.[20] As the rival institutional endeavours develop, they should be compared using forms of 'normal' discourse that include attempts to apply such criteria as cost, pupil interest, parental support, examination results, success in obtaining employment or moving on to higher education, confidence of pupils in finding things out on their own and so on over a fixed period of time, after which a decision regarding their futures might be made. It is not that such comparisons could ever be made precise but, as I have argued, it is an objectivist myth to suppose that present institutional comparison can be made precise. Theoretical progress may be made, however, not only when a set of institutional arrangements is judged not to have met the previously agreed conditions under which they might be continued but also when those who work within rival educational institutions are sufficiently attracted to each other's concrete successes that they come to visit each other and learn about each other's successes. In a Kuhnian manner, they may come to modify what they themselves do:

> No process quite like choice has occurred, but they are practising the new theory nonetheless.[21]

It should be noted that my proposal is not based on the idea that all centralization of decision-making is undesirable. We can come to prefer certain proposals over others by considering their merits in the contexts in which they will be implemented and that does not mean that all centrally-devised policies cannot usefully function as guides to particular practices. For me, the opposition between centrally and locally devised policies may be seen as another subset of the more general opposition between relativism and objectivism — oppositions that miss the point that theoretical progress comes about by individuals interpreting what each other is doing and coming to see how their endeavours might be improved rather than by assuming that the only valid policies are those that are derived locally or that the inter-

*tion and evaluation of centrally devised policies is any more problematic than their locally devised counterparts. For example, I imagine that it would be possible to outline a curriculum framework that could command widespread support and serve as a guide to curricular decision-making without deforming the endeavour of teaching by imposing externally set objectives that are supposed to detail when and how teachers should work. Such a framework may provide the focus of a form of 'normal' discourse about the curriculum and as such may function as another 'touchstone' against which institutional comparisons may be made.

A curriculum framework need not necessarily be conceived and established in such a form that debate about how to apply criteria becomes more important than the establishing of a fruitful dialogue between people, guided by a concern to achieve an 'ideal consensus'. Instead of the idea that educational improvements are brought about by the 'management' of curriculum change, we may envisage a curriculum framework within which teachers are given resources and the encouragement to devise their own curricular materials, to plan their own learning environment and to learn from each other in the supportive atmosphere brought about in an organizational structure that promotes practical discursive rationality. Institutions which are structured in this way may avoid the deformation of discourse that is alleged to occur within a 'line management' form of institutional organization and may enable people to discuss their genuine concerns rather than those concerns that they might feel would least interfere with their career prospects. The set of conditions under which such institutions might be disbanded could form a temporary set of common meanings that sustains the new institution by setting a horizon for its members in the formative stages of practical development.

I am not suggesting that a common curricular framework should not evolve within the endeavour of teaching and the conversations that teachers have with other kinds of worker. Instead, I suggest that, within certain parameters, particularly financial but also statutory and conventional in the sense that children work towards similar targets (and here it seems that external examinations with all their problems, may be more helpful than internal assessment in providing some 'touchstone' for theory-comparison), it should be possible to validate educational theories. Validation may never be conclusive in the sense that parents were consumers who by their choice of school would ultimately also be validating a theory or as if 'league tables' of examination results could be directly equated with the relative success of different managerial systems. However, parental preference, examination results, pupil preference and so on might all provide the 'touchstone' necessary for educational theory-comparison.

It might be objected that such a move would complicate the system considerably and make it difficult to understand. I am not suggesting, however, that every aspect of education should be changed at the same time. Rather I am suggesting that it is rational to put some aspect of the institutional structure of schools in jeopardy rather than to continue to try to implement a range of curricular developments all at once. For the latter can lead to a loss of a sense of community, a loss of meaning for so many of those terms which teachers use to explain to each other what they are trying to do that it becomes impossible to make sense of the idea of theoretical progress because the terms in which theories might be compared no longer exist.

The tragedy of the dominance of objectivism in educational theory is that it excludes consideration of many of the issues that affect what goes on in schools, for example the allocation of resources. Instead, the issues of resources, pay and conditions of service, are ruled out of the court of objectivistic educational theorizing and are left to periodic government review. It is as if educational theory were narrowly conceived as thinking about learning as a psychological or philosophical concept in abstraction from the actual context in which it takes place.

My proposal that educational theorists of the hermeneutic persuasion should endeavour to agree upon some 'touchstone' with educational theorists of the objectivistic persuasion is risky in the sense that either type of theorist may always invoke an '*ad hoc*' hypothesis[22] to explain away their rival's 'successes' and their own 'failures' as defined by the agreed 'touchstone'. Moreover, the distortive effects of the dominance of objectivism may always lead us to view a hermeneuticist's success as an instrumental attempt to achieve pre-set objectives, thus further reinforcing the dominance of objectivism. To put it in Lakatos's terms, the attempt to establish whether a 'research programme' whose 'hard core' is constituted by social theories based on a practical discursive conception of rationality is progressing may always be thwarted by the impossibility of our ever realizing that conception in practice and may simply serve as a means of further reinforcing the dominance of objectivism. However, it seems to me that these risks are worth taking. Objectivism may still be the most appropriate underpinning for our educational practices, but without our taking these risks I do not see how this claim can ever be subjected to scrutiny and potential refutation.

Notes and References

1   KUHN, T.S. (1977) *The Essential Tension.*
2   *Ibid.*, p. 226.
3   Recently some schools in the private sector in England have seen that it
    is advantageous to advertise the fact that they do not have to follow the
    'national curriculum' (see my note 5 below). This is in contrast to all
    schools in the state sector that have had this initiative thrust upon them.
    (see *Times Educational Supplement*, 2 March 1990.)
4   EDGLEY, R. (1980) 'Education, work and politics', p. 15.
5   This is the result of the 'Education Reform Act' 1988, HMSO; see
    MACLURE, S. (1988) *Guide to the 'Education Reform Act'*, Hodder.
6   WARNOCK, M. (1989) *A Common Policy for Education*, ch. 3.
7   As is very often the case, particularly with vocational qualifications like
    the ones discussed in my Chapter 2.
8   MACINTYRE, A. (1981) *After Virtue*, see pp. 187–94. MacIntyre presents a
    moral theory which depends upon a conception of the 'good life' in
    which external goods are subordinate to internal goods. In a recent essay
    titled 'Education, Liberalism and Human Good', J. and P. White (1986b)
    argue that MacIntyre's notion of a practice may 'provide us with the
    tools for beginning to construct a theory — or theories — of education
    which many would find attractive' (p. 162). While I have not drawn
    specific curricular implications from MacIntyre's work, it seems to me
    that J. and P. White are correct in their assertion that 'there is something
    immensely attractive about [a MacIntyrean education]. It incorporates so
    many of the more appealing features of different schools of thought
    while avoiding the difficulties which generally accompany them. It
    stresses breadth of experience yet without sacrificing commitment; it is
    thoroughly pupil-centred, but sees the pupil always as a member of a
    community; it is not excessively biased towards the intellectual and
    academic but by no means excluding them; it stresses both the whole
    person and engagement in particular activities; it gives the virtues a
    prominence which many would wish to see restored; it sees the vital
    importance of traditions, but does not imprison pupils within them; and
    so on' (p. 161). It seems to me that my third Gadamerian account of
    learning is essential to the realization of these ideals for, without it, it is
    not clear how pupils could free themselves from the initial range of
    practices in which they were inducted and make choices about which
    alternative practices are worth pursuing.
9   The idea of teaching as a practice has recently been given much promin-
    ence by LANGFORD, G. (1985) *Education, Persons and Society: A Philo-
    sophical Enquiry*. See the exchange between Langford and S.B. Brooke-
    Norris in the *Journal of the Philosophy of Education*, 20,2, pp. 227–43, 1986.
    See also D.E. COOPER's review of Langford's book in the same issue.
    Cooper criticizes Langford for holding that teaching both *is* a practice
    with a tradition and *should be* a practice with a tradition. Cooper points
    out that if teaching presently is a practice with a tradition, then 'tradi-
    tion' must be taken in a very weak sense since teaching seems recently to
    have been subject to the most radical changes. If, alternatively, Langford

supposes that teaching should become a practice within which greater regard should be paid to tradition then, Cooper points out, Langford would need to show how the practice of teaching is presently being deformed. This he does not do. Whereas I can respond to Cooper's criticism with my Gadamerian argument that presently the practice of teaching is being deformed by instrumentalism with undesirable educational consequences.

10   GADAMER, H.G. (1975a) *Truth and Method*, p. 289.

11   OAKESHOTT, M. (1959) *The Voice of Poetry in the Conversation of Mankind*.

12   Interestingly some philosophers have come recently to demand something similar from philosophy — that it becomes more relevant. See *The Guardian*, 19 August 1989, pp. 10–11 for a discussion of 'Revisioning Philosophy'.

13   For example, when W. KLAFKI (*Aspekte Kritisch-konstructiver Erziehungswissenschaft*, 1976, p. 60) states that the major product of an 'action research' project may be a 'discourse', I take him to mean that educational theory need not always be conceived as a text or a text-analogue that sets out a narrative. Instead, educational theory may be conceived as an endeavour that involves a dialectical relationship between thinking about what to do next and acting in solidarity with other participants in the 'discourse'. In this way, educational theory is concerned to foster a set of communal relations that are non-coercive and authentic. No one can know in advance the time at which the production of a narrative or the engagement of others in collaborative action is going to be most efficacious in furthering the 'discourse' towards the 'ideal speech situation'. Hence my idea of educational theory includes both the production of a narrative such as this book and changing one's practical orientation through conversation with others.

14   WHITE, J.P. (1982) *The Aims of Education Restated*.

15   PETERS, R.S. (1966) *Ethics and Education*, ch. 2.

16   cf. TAYLOR, C. (1985) *Philosophical Papers*, vol. 2, especially chs. 1 and 3.

17   Gadamer, for example, writes 'The point is that genuine solidarity, authentic community should be realized', 1981, p. 80. The affinities between Gadamer, Habermas and Rorty are discussed by BERNSTEIN, R.J., 1983, see especially pp. 224–6.

18   We may draw an analogy between natural scientific and educational theory to illustrate this suggestion: just as theoretical physics progresses because experimental physics keeps pace with it and provides the means of checking theoretical predictions and continuing the 'scientific conversation', so educational theory may progress because institutional practices keep pace with it and continue the 'conversation of mankind'.

19   LAKATOS, I. (1978) *The Methodology of Scientific Research Programmes*.

20   Interestingly it is was reported in the *Independent on Sunday*, 18 February 1990, p. 41, that two 'sink' schools had been transformed into 'magnet' schools by changing the management ethos away from hierarchy towards greater democratic participation in decision-making.

21   KUHN, T.S. (1977) *The Essential Tension*, p. 339.

22   I am thinking here of the kind of considerations put forward by POPPER, K.R., 1957, which were discussed in my Chapters 3 and 5.

Conclusion

In the course of this study I have examined some theoretical origins
and educational implications of the philosophical notion of objectivism. In addition, I have tried to work out and explain the implications
of an alternative to this notion. To conclude, I speculate first on some
of the things that might be expected to happen if objectivism continues to dominate educational policy, and second on some of the
likely implications of a challenge to the dominance of objectivism.

Objectivism Continued

We have seen how the empiricist idea of a permanent external world
that can be mapped by certain propositions gives rise to the objectivistic idea that there is a permanent neutral set of criteria to which we
can appeal in order to determine what we should do and how we
should think. Objectivists might argue that even though we do not
yet have access to these ultimate criteria, the continuing attempt to
formulate and apply criteria is our best guide to rationality. Hence
objectivists are suspicious of the notion of practical knowledge. This
notion presents the most serious and obvious threat to their project
and they attempt to remove that threat in two ways. First, they
suggest that by following a set of rules and/or criteria, people can
learn all that there is to know. In that way practical knowledge is
supposed to be completely described. Second, they distinguish between policy, theory and practice. Policy is supposed by objectivists
to prescribe the aims of practice and theory is supposed to detail the
most efficient way of achieving those aims. Hence it does not matter
so much how something is done as long as it is done at minimum

cost. Cost provides the ultimate criterion for objectivists since mini-mizing cost is amenable to mathematical decidability.

The formulation of educational aims is informed by the notion of a market and managers are supposed to ensure that market demand is ascertained, described and shown to be satisfied at minimum cost. Within this formulation teachers increasingly work as technicians using 'student centred' materials prepared for them and promoted by 'theorists'. Presently a worry about future employment abetted by government rhetoric fuels a strong vocational impetus to market demand — enterprise education, education for business, industrial studies, work experience[1] and so on, are developments that embody the idea of people being most interested in getting a job and earning their living. Now, as I have argued, none of these developments are necessarily undesirable by themselves. Of course people are interested in earning their living and it may well be the case that learning how businesses operate is an important curricular component. However, taken together these innovations may constitute such an attack on those settled forms of discourse that sustain the educational endeavour as it used to be conceived generally, that systematic evaluation of developments becomes very difficult. Moreover, the dominance of objectivism works against such evaluation partly through the empiri-cist idea that tradition hinders progress but also through the idea that educational policy is founded on the secure foundation of market demand that is something empirically determined and value-neutral.

Should these innovations continue apace, fuelled as they might be by worries about overall economic performance, then we may expect some governments further to attempt to raise the status of the voca-tional aspects of our curricular network. This attempt embraces the objectivistic idea of a vocational preparation and vocationally prepared students are awarded qualifications that used to be reserved for suc-cessful academic study. I can see no limit to the type of jobs that might be deemed to be amenable to a degree-level preparation. However, if a vocational preparation means little other than the limitation of study to those things that are objectively related to a particular job, then there may well be a case for re-establishing the distinction between the vocational and the academic as a subset of a distinction between practice and theory. Many would find this con-sequence of the dominance of objectivism within education to be unfortunate. For them, the distinction between the academic and the vocational, like the distinction between the arts and the sciences, is not so important as the distinction between interest across our network of endeavours and the attempt to limit that interest to a particular endeavour. The former type of interest may well be essential in *all* kinds of study.

An objectivistic conception of vocationalism leads ultimately to the conflation of educational and commercial institutions. We have seen some moves in this direction already.[2] If state schools and colleges are underfunded then there is a temptation if not an imperative for these institutions to compensate for a financial deficiency by expanding 'enterprise activities'. Not only might such expansion turn a 'loss' into a 'profit', but also it might reasonably be claimed that those schools and colleges with a good record of commercial success are likely to turn out people who have a good chance of promoting their own or someone else's commercial success. Overall economic performance might be expected to improve as such 'educands' become 'workers'.[3] In turn, objectivists of this persuasion might claim that while educational inequalities are inevitable, at least inequality may be based on something observable, namely material possessions. It could be argued that it is preferable to base inequalities on observable and easily describable criteria than on some notion of educational need[4] that is difficult if not impossible to quantify.

However, we have seen that objectivism is impossible: the 'market' is not a value-neutral device for determining policy in education, nor is the emphasis on vocationalism and managerialism that cohere with consumerism well placed. Yet objectivism dominates and limits theorizing to an investigation of the most efficient way of achieving the aims of educational policy, rather than offering a fundamental critique of the policy itself. We may expect an increasingly hierarchical managerial structure to sustain this fundamentally flawed philosophy of education. In effect, an illusion of objectivity may be maintained when a hierarchical group has such complete control over its members and their activities that a common interpretation of educational policy can be presented for others to follow. Criticism becomes limited to 'puzzle solving' — eliminating minor incoherence within a general framework for development that is accepted by a coterie of managers who share common values and prior suppositions. Managers may be pressurized into equating loyalty with an uncritical adherence to certain values and norms. Hence we may end up with a management structure that reflects a very limited form of discourse and we may observe an increasing use of the power of patronage and finance to sustain a form of discourse within which 'external goods' dominate. One correspondent suggested that even now the power of patronage might extend from the present British Government downwards. He commented that:

it is deeply reassuring to have it confirmed that the leaders of the academic world have justly earnt a 'higher than average profile in this years New Years Honours list' ... Would it be possible (from say 1991) to distinguish explicitly a) those awarded honours for the defence of academic virtues from b) those who have been able to combine the fearless pursuit of truth with being 'hired prizefighters' for H.M. Government?[5]

At the bottom of this hierarchy we may find a real point of tension between objectivism and a practical discursive conception of rationality. Here teachers may find themselves trying to reconcile the imposition of a form of authority that is embedded within a hierarchical management structure with a struggle to establish their own authority that is embedded within a practical discursive conception of rationality which supports a view of learning that goes beyond vocationalism. Between top and bottom of the hierarchy we may expect to find small groups of managers trying to reconcile the objectivistic policy statements and interpretations which they are charged to promote with the maintenance of personal relationships that enable them to motivate their 'subordinates'. This reconciliation may be impossible because many people do not feel comfortable with the idea that their collegial relationships are little more than a technique or device for the 'morally neutral' attempt to implement educational policy. Nor might many teachers feel comfortable with a proliferation of policy statements all purporting to prescribe the actions that they should take. This discomfort is likely to be particularly apparent if a proliferation of advisers and inspectors are appointed to guide and assess the way that teachers interpret policy directives.

In this climate three options might appear to be open to teachers. The first is to move up the hierarchy away from teaching. The second is to become 'morally neutral' technicians themselves by acting as a 'resource' upon which students can draw as they work individually through material that has been compiled by others and that is, in one sense, the end point of objectivistic educational policy. The third is successfully to set up a business within school under the auspices of one of the so-called 'enterprise initiatives'. However, it is not clear that such entrepreneurs are teaching in the sense that many of us understand and approve. In all cases we seem to be left with an impoverished education system. Of course this impoverishment is not likely to be immediately noticeable. There are many good experienced teachers within the system who simply could refuse to adopt what we might call the technique of 'worksheet completion', despite the pressures that might be put upon them to do so. These teachers are able enough to interest their students in a wider conception of learning. Moreover, there is some evidence to suggest that students recognize and value this form of teaching.[6] However, the longer that objectivism continues to dominate, the heavier the odds are stacked against those whose effort is directed towards ends that cannot be described in behavioural terms and towards the idea that practical knowledge is an essential, valuable yet unformalizable type of knowledge. The tradition that sustains such teaching is under threat and we may be deprived of an important endeavour against which to validate other attempts to educate.

Objectivism Challenged

To allow a range of alternative endeavours to flourish may be our best guarantee against the uncritical adoption of any particular idea, policy or practice. We may provide more opportunities to learn from each other in the supportive atmosphere that is brought about in a noncoercive environment which recognizes that progress and development cannot always nor usually be quantified in the short term. In summary, we might shift the emphasis away from managerialism back towards teaching.[7]

In the introduction I argued that a transformative curriculum theory should be located within the same theoretical framework that currently informs educational practice. To challenge objectivism and the ideas of vocationalism, managerialism and consumerism that cohere with it is not to reject all aspects of those ideas. Instead, such a challenge may transform those ideas by promoting one of them further. Consumerism may offer the best possibility for mounting a challenge to objectivism because a form of liberalism is built into the notion of the market. Given the choice, people may prefer something like the alternative philosophy of education that I outlined in Chapter 6. Paradoxically, I believe that by promoting the idea of a free market in education which includes a sort of free market in ideas, objectivism may be transformed.

However, even though Conservative governments on both sides of the Atlantic have been keen to adopt the idea of an educational market, to date only certain aspects of education have been subjected to the rigours of market demand. There are of course good reasons for this: for example, even if students wanted astrology or pornography in the curriculum, it is doubtful whether responsible governments would equate wants with needs in this case. Similarly, even though some governments are keen to promote local management of educational institutions, the legal changes that are necessary for a practical discursive conception of rationality to flourish within some educational institutions have not been made. Yet it is this change that could enable objectivism to be challenged.[8]

Let us consider four immediate benefits to educational institutions within the state sector that might be anticipated, should government control of education be liberalized. First, many of the curricular initiatives that have been imposed upon state schools and colleges could be avoided. Second, the tyranny of endless internal assessments and elaborate attempts to raise the status of awards based on internal assessments may be avoided.[9] Should governments impose internal assessment upon the state sector while the private sector is free to adopt some external norm referenced examinations, then not only are some teachers handicapped by the administrative burden that is incurred with internal assessment, but also an important touchstone for the evaluation of private and state sector education is lost. Private education may be perceived to be better than it actually is because publicly observable success rate in high status external examinations will always be rated more highly by objectivists than estimations of progress that are based on intuition or 'professional judgment'. Third, an interpretive conception of educational theory might be instituted so that teachers were encouraged to be theoretical instead of technical. If my arguments are correct then this would be the most obvious benefit of some loosening of government control in education.

I take education to be a set of interrelated endeavours, such as the endeavour of teaching along with certain institutional endeavours like administration. I take it too that educational endeavours are related to a wider set of endeavours which people are either interested in learning about or which affect the way that they conceive of what they are doing. Philosophy of education is theorizing in the sense that it seeks to understand and explain what those involved in the educational enterprise are doing, with the purpose of bringing greater coherence to the way in which educational endeavours relate to one another. That means finding new and more interesting ways of speaking and acting in education (rather similar to Goodman's notion of the different 'ways of worldmaking'),[10] on making connections between different forms of practical discourse, and on thinking up ways to reinterpret what we do, with the aim of framing the various options that we face and of giving us the theory that will function as 'touchstone' in our adjudication and evaluation of the differences between them.

The familiarity of philosophers with different ways of world-making and different ways of viewing the language–thought–reality relationship makes them particularly suited to taking a leading role in an activity that is concerned with getting others to find more fruitful ways of speaking and acting, making connections between types of discourse and reinterpreting their predicament. I do not wish, however, to suggest that educational theory is the sole preserve of philosophy of education or *vice-versa*. In my view nothing much hinges on whether educational theorists are primarily interested in philosophy, psychology, action research or whatever. What matters is that it becomes more acceptable to theorize about education from perspectives other than that of objectivism.

The hermeneutic idea of a constant critical reinterpretation of theory into practice and practice into theory seems to me to be not only preferable to the dominant 'theory guiding practice' paradigm of educational theory but also to the more sophisticated forms of what I described as the 'move to practice'. According to my thesis, it is possible to be theoretical without any immediate regard for so-called 'practical' problems and that is about as disinterested as anyone can be. Even though theorizing relates to practical problems it can never merely be a response to them nor does theorizing ever necessarily offer any immediate solutions to immediate problems. Nevertheless, it may still be desirable to free some people from immediate practical concerns in order that they might devote more of their attention to theorizing in the hope that the educational endeavour might be improved. This proposal may be validated in the same way as any other proposal — that is by the setting up of different institutional structures with common criteria of success and waiting to see what happens.

The fourth benefit could accrue if enthusiasm for the idea of a vocational preparation were tempered in favour of a general concern with the theoretical for all types of worker. Let us see how preparation for a particular vocation — teaching — might be organized if government control of teacher training were to be loosened. This example may serve to illustrate how the idea of a vocational preparation generally might be implemented. The empiricist 'theory guiding practice' idea gave rise to the institutionalization of a particular version of theory within colleges of vocational education generally and colleges and departments of education in particular. The hermeneutic idea that theory and practice are like conversational partners suggests that teacher education should be more closely related to the practical teaching context. While it is possible for tutors within colleges and departments of education to create a context within which useful preparatory work for teaching practice can be carried out by trainee teachers, using micro-teaching equipment, planning lessons, reviewing curriculum content and so on, such preparation is always subject to the criticism that 'practice lessons' bear little resemblance to those lessons that trainees are supposed to present in schools.

As a result of this type of criticism there have been moves towards including more 'school experience' in teacher training courses — and there are good reasons to suppose that these moves will continue to gain momentum. Moreover, there might be great advantage to be gained if 'school experience' were largely to replace those parts of the teacher training curriculum that are presently concerned with simulating that 'experience' and if teachers themselves were to become more involved in teacher training. There have been various suggestions as to how this might be organized, ranging from M. Warnock's idea of the 'teacher tutor' and a 'General Teaching Council'[11] to the procedure whereby the trainee teacher might work with a variety of teachers in a variety of schools on a sort of rotational basis, or indeed a combination of both.

The move in this direction was given some momentum in the White Paper 'Teaching Quality'.[12] However, my thesis suggests a more radical break with the institutional arrangements suggested by the Secretaries of State when they recommend that

> the staff of training institutions who are concerned with pedagogy should have school teaching experience. They should have enjoyed recent success as teachers in the age range to which their training courses are directed.[13]

It may be preferable for all pedagogical matters to be dealt with in school and for teacher trainers largely to renounce their claims to having something special to say to trainee teachers about pedagogy on the basis of their supposed theoretical awareness. That is not to say that the 'theory of pedagogy' should be given up. Rather it is to say that no theory of pedagogy is ever likely to replace the sort of apprenticeship that a trainee teacher might get by working along with an experienced colleague.[14]

The dominance of objectivism sees to it that teacher trainees pass through the tutelage of so-called educational theorists as a preparation for their future careers and many 'theorists' tend to conceive the problem of the relationship between theory and practice as a search for the ways in which their tutelage is appropriate to the preparation of teachers rather than the logically prior issue as to whether their tutelage is appropriate. Professional studies[15] might be seen as the latest in a series of attempts to bridge a divide that had only opened up because the institutionalization of an epistemological framework resulted in some studies being validated within an academic context, and others being validated in a vocational context.[16]

If teachers were themselves to take over the training of their trainees, then there would remain the question of the most appropriate institutional arrangements for enabling those who are charged with the special responsibility for theorizing about education critically to interpret the work of teachers and others involved in the educational enterprise and *vice-versa*. It should be remembered that my proposal for some people to be freed from immediate practical concerns in order to search for coherence across a range of endeavours was not based on any academic division of labour but simply on the ungrounded hope that better progress in educational theory might be made if such a proposal were implemented. However, if educational theorists were to accept the task of looking at the ways that teachers interpret what they are doing against a range of different considerations, one of the most important being financial, then we might have available a range of properly costed proposals with which to debate our educational priorities and with which to appraise any new developments. We would not have to assume that every new development that seemed to have some attractive features was necessarily any better than the last. It may be that such an arrangement might lead to the production of a series of arguments that give quite specific support to one course of action as opposed to another. My thesis, however, leaves room for the view that such an engagement with theory might change the teacher's orientation in a way that it would be foolish of me to try to predict.

It follows that colleges and departments of education should have a much broader range of research interests than is presently the case.[17] Instead of the present dominance of psychology as the discipline supposedly most concerned with educational measurement, curriculum development and the theoretical underpinnings of pedagogy, educational policy too might be offered and made one of the main thrusts of educational research, not as an after-thought, but as an integral part of debate about the purpose of education, the desirability of certain sorts of society and the relations between education and other influences which impinge on people's lives. If training in pedagogy is best left to teachers themselves, then it follows that those institutions responsible for educational theory could be much smaller than is presently the case. There seems to be a need for a staff-college element within such institutions that would encourage the continuing engagement of teachers with theory. Some exchange of teachers and theorists between institutions may be desirable in order to increase the mutual understanding of what teachers and theorists think that they are doing, but not to pretend that a term's secondment in schools is ever likely to ensure that teacher trainers have 'enjoyed recent success as teachers'.

The proposed wide remit for those institutions that might be charged with the special responsibility for educational theory is not meant to imply that such institutions should be the final arbiters about which way the state education system should develop, as if educational debate would be removed from the political sphere and as if teacher and employer associations would be unnecessary. Instead, educational theorists might outline the prices to be paid for various developments[18] and in that way might enable people to maximize the coherence of their networks of endeavour on the basis of carefully constructed arguments and exemplary practice. Hence it is worth hoping that the arguments of some educational theorists, at any rate, should be endorsed on the basis of the acceptability of some of their previous attempts to theorize. I accept that theory can never determine an outcome. However, it is worth hoping that it might influence the discussion in a particular direction.

Notes and References

1   See, for example, *Mini-Enterprises in Schools 1989/90 a DTI project supported by National Westminster Bank*, not dated, University of Warwick; MARSDEN, C. (1989) *Why Business Should Work With Education*, B.P. Educational Service; *Training and Enterprise Councils*, Business in the Community, City Rd, London, 1989; *The Enterprise Initiative*, Department of Trade and Industry, HMSO, Dd8221570INDYJO816NJ; *Education at Work: A Guide for Schools: Work Experience and Related Activities for Pupils under 16*, Department of Education and Science, 1988, HMSO Dd8172081EDUCJO333RP.

2   *Ibid.*

3   The Local Management of Schools Initiative was proposed in the 1988 Education Reform Act (see my note 5 in the previous chapter) and may be the first step in the way of further commercialism in schools. Already some schools have built up quite large businesses within their curricula.

4   A rugged individualism seems to underpin the continuation of an educational policy that is of most interest to objectivists. However, as many have argued, there seems to be collective needs for certain things including the need for a public forum within which debate about the nature of

such needs can take place. See IGNATIEFF, M. (1984) *The Needs of Strangers.*

5 HARTNETT, A., 'Letter', *Times Higher Education Supplement*, 12 January 1990, p. 12.

6 See WRINGE, C. (1988) *Understanding Educational Aims*, esp. ch. 1.

7 To put this in MacIntyre's terms we might shift the emphasis away from 'external' towards 'internal' goods, MACINTYRE, A. (1981) *After Virtue*; see also my Ch. 2.

8 This change would also facilitate 'action research' though I believe that my account of educational theory goes beyond the one assumed by many 'action researchers'.

9 Awards based on external norm-referenced examinations seem to enjoy far higher status than awards based on internally assessed criterion-referenced continuous assessments and seem to impose less of an administrative burden upon teachers.

10 GOODMAN, N. (1978) *Ways of Worldmaking.*

11 WARNOCK, M. 'Teacher teach thyself', The 1985 Richard Dimbleby Lecture, printed in *The Listener*, 28 March 1985, pp. 10–14.

12 'Teaching Quality', White Paper, Cmnd 8836, March 1983, HMSO.

13 'Initial Teacher Training: Approval of Courses', Circular No 3/84, DES, 13 April 1984, p. 6.

14 cf. JONATHAN, R. (1981) 'Empirical research and educational theory', in SIMON, B. and WILLCOCKS, J. (Eds) *Research and Practice in the Primary Classroom*, pp. 161–75.

15 Presently teacher education might be seen to be comprised of two components, one concerned with pedagogy, the other concerned with educational theory, where educational theory is often conceived to be concerned with something approaching an immersion into the 'disciplines'. (cf. ALEXANDER, R.J. (1984) 'Innovation and continuity in the initial teacher education curriculum', in ALEXANDER, R.J., CRAFT, M. and LYNCH, J. (Eds) *Change in Teacher Education* especially pp. 113–46.) It is worth noting that 'curriculum studies' tends to have a foot in both camps, so to speak, and is often used as a supposed bridge between educational theory and practice. Recently 'professional studies' have come to replace 'curriculum studies' as a bridge between theory and practice — 'old wine in new bottles' as one commentator puts it (ALEXANDER, R.J., 1984, p. 137). The discussion of the professional studies issue occurs throughout the collection edited by ALEXANDER, R.J. *et al.*, 1984. See also FOSS, K. (1975) *The Status of Professional Studies in Teacher Education*, University of Sussex, Education Area Occasional Paper 4.

16 Again this is discussed throughout the collection edited by Alexander *et al.*, 1984, and Alexander discusses the influences on the academic/vocational division in his 'Innovation and continuity in the initial teacher education curriculum', pp. 103–60.

17 This argument suggests that it might be preferable if educational theory took account of developments in other types of theory. A polytechnic-type institution might facilitate such exchange of views.

18 cf. JONATHAN, R. (1985) 'Education, philosophy of education and context'.

Bibliography

The Bibliography contains entries of two sorts:

(i)   works to which reference has been made in the course of the text;
(ii) works which are not specifically referred to in the course of the text but which have close relevance.

The following abreviations are used:

JCS   *Journal of Curriculum Studies*
JFHE   *Journal of Further and Higher Education*
JPE   *Journal of Philosophy of Education*
NFER   *National Foundation for Educational Research*
PESGB   *Proceedings of the Philosophy of Education Society of Great Britain*
RKP   Routledge and Kegan Paul

ADORNO, T.W. (1982) *Against Epistemology: A Metacritique*, Oxford, Blackwell.
AINLEY, P. (1988) *From School to YTS*, Milton Keynes, Open University Press.
ALEXANDER, R.J., CRAFT, M. and LYNCH, J. (1984) *Change in Teacher Education*, Holt, Rinehart and Winston.
APPLE, M.W. (1986) *Teachers and Texts*, RKP.
ARCHAMBAULT, R.D. (Ed.) (1965) *Philosophical Analysis and Education*, RKP.
ARNOWITZ, S. and GIROUX, H.A. (1986) *Education under Siege*, RKP.
ASPIN, D.N. (1980) *Comparable Education* 16, 2, pp. 171–8.
ASPIN, D.N. (1982) 'Philosophy of education', in COHEN, L., THOMAS, J. and MANION, L., *Educational Research and Development in Britain 1970–1980*, NFER, Nelson.
BARROW, R. (1981) *Journal of Curriculum Studies*, 13, 4, p. 371.
BARROW, R. (1984) *Giving Teaching Back to Teachers*, Brighton, Wheatsheaf.
BAUMAN, Z. (1978) *Hermeneutics and Social Science*, Hutchinson.
BERNSTEIN, R.J. (1976) *The Restructuring of Social and Political Theory*, Oxford, Blackwell.
BERNSTEIN, R.J. (1983) *Beyond Objectivism and Relativism*, Oxford, Blackwell.

BERNSTEIN, R.J. (Ed.) (1985) *Habermas and Modernity*, Oxford, Blackwell.

BHASKAR, R. (1979) *The Possibility of Naturalism*, Brighton, Harvester.

BLOOM, B.S. (1956) *Taxonomy of Educational Objectives* in 2 vols, New York, David Mckay and Co.

BLOOR, D. (1983) *Wittgenstein: A Social theory of Knowledge*, Macmillan.

BODEN, M. (1977) *Artificial Intelligence and Natural Man*, Brighton, Harvester.

BOWLES, S. and GINTIS, H. (1976) *Schooling in Capitalist America*, RKP.

BRENT, A. (1978) *Philosophical Foundations for the Curriculum*, Allen and Unwin.

BROCK-UTNE, B. (1980) 'What is educational action research?' *CARN* Bulletin no. 4, p. 10.

BROWNHILL, R. (1983) *Education and the Nature of Knowledge*, Croom Helm.

CANTOR, L.M. and ROBERTS, I.F. (1979) *Further Education Today*, RKP.

CARNEGIE COUNCIL ON POLICY STUDIES IN HIGHER EDUCATION (1979) *Giving Youth a Better Chance*, Jossey-Bass.

CARR, W. (1980) 'The gap between theory and practice', *JFHE*, 4,1, pp. 60–9.

CARR, W. (1983) 'Can educational research be scientific?', *JPE*, 17,1, pp. 35–43.

CARR, W. (1985) 'Review of educational theory and its foundation disciplines', *JCS*, 17,1.

CARR, W. (1986) 'Theories of theory and practice', *JPE*, 20, 2, pp. 177–85.

CARR, W. (1989) 'The idea of an educational science', *JPE*, 23,1, pp. 29–37.

CARR, W. and KEMMIS, S. (1983) *Becoming Critical: Knowing Through Action Research*, Victoria, Deakin University Press.

DAVIDSON, D. (1984) *Inquiries into Truth and Interpretation*, Oxford, Clarendon Press.

DEARDEN, R.F. (1984) *Theory and Practice in Education*, RKP.

DEARDEN, R.F., HIRST, P.H. and PETERS, R.S. (Eds) (1972) *Educational and the Development of Reason*, RKP.

DILTHEY, W. (Ed.) (1976) *Selected Writing*, Rickman H.P. Cambridge.

DOCKRELL, W. and HAMILTON, D. (Eds) (1980) *Rethinking Educational Research*, Hodder and Stoughton.

EARL, P.E. (1983) *The Economic Imagination: Towards a Behavioural Analysis of Choice*, Brighton, Wheatsheaf.

EARL, P.E. (1984) *The Corporate Imagination*, Brighton, Wheatsheaf.

EDGLEY, R. (1969) *Reason in Theory and Practice*, Hutchinson.

EDGLEY, R. (1980) 'Education, work and politics', *JPE*, 14,1, pp. 3–16.

EDWARDS, J.C. (1982) *Ethics without Philosophy: Wittgenstein and the Moral Life*, University Press of Florida.

EVERS, C.W. (1982) Logical Structure and Justification in Educational Theory. Unpublished PhD thesis, Department of Education, University of Sydney.

EVERS, C.W. and WALKER, J.C. (1984) *Epistemology, Semantics and Educational Theory*, Occasional Paper no 16, Department of Education, University of Sydney.

FANN, K.T. (1969) *Wittgenstein's Conception of Philosophy*, Berkeley, University of California Press.

FEYERABEND, P.K. (1975) *Against Method*, Humanities Press.
FEYERABEND, P.K. (1978) *Science in a Free Society*, New Left Books.
FOSS, K. (1975) *The Status of Professional Studies in Teacher Education*, University of Sussex, Education Area Occasional Paper 4.
GADAMER, H.G. (1970) 'Replik', *Continuum*, 8.
GADAMER, H.G. (1975a) *Truth and Method*, Sheed and Ward.
GADAMER, H.G. (1975b) 'Hermeneutics and social science', *Cultural Hermeneutics*, 2.
GADAMER, H.G. (1976) *Philosophical Hermeneutics*, Berkeley, University of California Press.
GADAMER, H.G. (1981) *Reason in the Age of Science*, Cambridge, Mass, M.I.T. Press.
GADAMER, H.G. (1985) *Philosophical Apprenticeships*, Cambridge, Mass, M.I.T. Press.
GARFINKEL, A. (1981) *Forms of Explanation*, New Haven, Yale University Press.
GELLNER, E. (1968) *Words and Things*, Pelican.
GELLNER, E. (1973) *Cause and Meaning in the Social Sciences*, RKP.
GELLNER, E. (1974) *Legitimation of Belief*, Cambridge University Press.
GELLNER, E. (1979) *Spectacles and Predicaments*, Cambridge University Press.
GELLNER, E. (1985) *Relativism and Social Science*, Cambridge University Press.
GEUSS, R. (1981) *The Idea of a Critical Theory*, Cambridge University Press.
GIDDENS, A. (1976) *New Rules of Sociological Method*, Hutchinson.
GIDDENS, A. (1977) *Studies in Social and Political Theory*, Hutchinson.
GIDDENS, A. (1982) *Sociology: A Brief but Critical Introduction*, Macmillan.
GLEESON, D. and MARDLE, G. (1980) *Further Education or Training?* RKP.
GOLBY, M., Greenwald, J. and WEST, R. (Eds) (1975) *Curriculum Design*, Croom Helm.
GOODMAN, N. (1978) *Ways of Worldmaking*, Brighton, Harvester.
GOODMAN, N. (1984) *Of Mind and Other Matters*, Harvard University Press.
GROSS, B. and GROSS, R. (Eds) (1985) *The Great School Debate*, New York, Simon and Schuster Inc.
GRUNDY, S. (1987) *Curriculum: Product or Praxis*, Lewes, Falmer Press.
HAACK, S. (1978) *Philosophy of Logics*, Cambridge University Press, especially pp. 112–22.
HABERMAS, J. (1970) 'Towards a theory of communicative competence', *Recent Sociology*, 2, pp. 115–48, New York, McMillan.
HABERMAS, J. (1971) *Towards a Rational Society*, Heinemann.
HABERMAS, J. (1972) *Knowledge and Human Interests*, Heinemann.
HABERMAS, J. (1973) 'A postscript to knowledge and human interests', *Philosophy and the Social Sciences*, 3, pp. 157–89.
HABERMAS, J. (1974) *Theory and Practice*, Heinemann.
HABERMAS, J. (1975) 'On systematically distorted communication', *Inquiry*, 13, pp. 205–18.
HABERMAS, J. (1976) *Legitimation Crisis*, p. 113.
HABERMAS, J. (1977) 'A review of Gadamer's truth and method', in DALLMAYR, F. and McCARTHY, T. (Eds) *Understanding and Social Inquiry*, Notre Dame, Ind, University of Notre Dame Press, pp. 335–63.

HABERMAS, J. (1984) *The Theory of Communicative Action*, Vol 1, Heinemann.

HAHN, F. and HOLLIS, M. (Eds) (1979) *Philosophy and Economic Theory*, Oxford University Press.

HAMLYN, D.W. (1970) *The Theory of Knowledge*, Macmillan.

HARRIS, K. (1979) *Education and Knowledge*, RKP.

HARTNETT, A. 'Letter', *Times Higher Education Supplement*, 12 January 1990, p. 12.

HARTNETT, A. and NAISH, M. (Eds) (1976) *Theory and Practice of Education*, in 2 vols, Heinemann.

HAYES, C., IZATT, A., MORRISON, J., SMITH, H. and TOWNSEND, C. (1982) *Foundation Training Issues*, Institute of Manpower Studies, University of Sussex.

HEIDEGGER, M. (1962) *Being and Time*, New York, Harper and Row.

HELD, D. (1980) *Introduction to Critical Theory*, Hutchinson.

HESSE, M. (1980) *Revolutions and Reconstructions in the Philosophy of Science*, Brighton, Harvester.

HIRST, P.H. (1974) *Knowledge and the Curriculum*, RKP.

HIRST, P.H. (Ed.) (1983) *Educational Theory and its Foundation Disciplines*, RKP.

HIRST, P.H. and PETERS, R.S. (1970) *The Logic of Education*, RKP.

HOLLAND, R.F. (1980) *Against Empiricism*, Oxford, Blackwell.

HOLLIS, M. and LUKES, S. (1982) *Rationality and Relativism*, Oxford, Blackwell.

HOLT, M. (1983) 'Vocationalism: The new threat to universal education', *Forum*, Summer Issue, pp. 84–6.

HOLT, M. (Ed.) (1987) *Skills and Vocationalism: The Easy Answer*, Croom Helm.

HOOKWAY, C. and PETTIT, P. (1978) *Action and Interpretation*, Cambridge University Press.

HORKHEIMER, M. (1972) *Critical Theory*, New York, Herder and Herder.

HOWARD, R.J. (1982) *Three Faces of Hermeneutics*, Berkeley, University of California Press.

HOY, D.C. (1978) *The Critical Circle*, Berkeley, University of California Press.

HUMES, W. (1986) *The Leadership Class in Scottish Education*, John Donald.

IGNATIEFF, M. (1984) *The Needs of Strangers*, Chatto.

JOHNSTON, R. (1984) *Occupational Training Families: Their implications for FE*, FEU.

JONATHAN, R.M. (1981) Educational Theory: Its Nature, Scope and Limits. PhD thesis, University of Leicester.

JONATHAN, R.M. (1983) 'The manpower service model of education', *Cambridge Journal of Education*.

JONATHAN, R.M. (1985) 'Education, philosophy of education and context', *JPE*, 19,1.

JONATHAN, R.M. (1987) 'Core Skills in the Youth Training Scheme: An educational analysis', in HOLT, M., 1987, *op cit*.

KATZNELSON, I. and WEIR, M. (1985) *Schooling for All*, New York, Basic Books.

KLAFKI, W. (1974) 'Handlungsforschung', in WULF, I. (Ed.) *Wörterbuch der Erziehung*, Verlag, München, R. Piper and Co.

KLAFKI, W. (1976) *Aspekte kritisch-konstructiver Erziehungswissenschaft*, Weinheim and Basel, Beltz Verlag.

KRIPKE, S.A. (1982) *Wittgenstein: On Rules and Private Language*, Oxford, Blackwell.

KUHN, T.S. (1962) *The Structure of Scientific Revolutions*, University of Chicago Press (second enlarged edition, 1970).

KUHN, T.S. (1977) *The Essential Tension*, University of Chicago Press.

LAKATOS, I. (1978) *Mathematics, Science and Epistemology*, Cambridge University Press.

LAKATOS, I. (1978) *The Methodology of Scientific Research Programmes*, Cambridge University Press.

LAKATOS, I. and MUSGRAVE, A. (Eds) (1970) *Criticism and the Growth of Knowledge*, Cambridge University Press.

LANGFORD, G. and O'CONNOR, D.J. (1973) *New Essays in the Philosophy of Education*, RKP.

LANGFORD, G. (1985) *Education, Persons and Society: A Philosophical Enquiry*, Macmillan.

LASLETT, P. and RUNCIMAN, W.G. (Eds) (1962) *Philosophy Politics and Society*, Oxford, Blackwell.

LLOYD, D.I. (1976) 'Theory and practice', *PESGB*, 10, p. 110.

LOUCH, A.R. (1966) *Explanation and Human Action*, Oxford University Press.

MACE, J. (1984) *Higher Education Review*, Summer, pp. 39–56.

MacINTYRE, A. (1981) *After Virtue*, Duckworth.

MacLURE, S. (1988) *Guide to the 'Education Reform Act'*, Hodder and Stoughton.

MALCOLM, N. (1972) *Problems of Mind: Descartes to Wittgenstein*, Allen and Unwin.

MAGER, R.F. (1962) *Preparing Instructional Objectives*, Belmont California, Fearon;

MATTHEWS, M.R. (1980) *The Marxist Theory of Schooling*, Brighton, Harvester.

McCARTHY, T. (1973) 'A theory of communicative competence', *Philosophy of the Social Sciences*, iii, p. 140.

McCARTHY, T. (1978) *The Critical Theory of Jürgen Habermas*, Hutchinson.

MILL, J.S. (1859) *Utilitarianism, Liberty and Representative Government*, Dent Everyman.

MOORE, G.E. (1959) *Philosophical Papers*, Allen and Unwin.

MOORE, T.W. (1974) *Educational Theory: An Introduction*, RKP.

OAKESHOTT, M. (1959) *The Voice of Poetry in the Conversation of Mankind*, Bowes and Bowes.

OAKESHOTT, M. (1962) *Rationalism in Politics*, Methuen.

OAKESHOTT, M. (1975) *On Human Conduct*, Oxford, Clarendon Press.

O'CONNOR, D.J. (1957) *An Introduction to the Philosophy of Education*, RKP.

O'CONNOR, D.J. (1973) 'The nature and scope of educational theory (1)', in LANGFORD, G. and O'CONNOR, D.J. *op cit*.

O'CONNOR, D.J. (1982) 'Two concepts of education', *JPE*, 16,2, pp. 137–46.

PAPERT, S. (1980) *Mindstorms: Children, Computers, and Powerful Ideas*, Brighton, Harvester.

PETERS, R.S. (1966) *Ethics and Education*, Allen and Unwin.

PETERS, R.S. (Ed.) (1967) *The Concept of Education*, RKP.

PETERS, R.S. (1977) *Philosophy and the Education of Teachers*, RKP.

PITCHER, G. (Ed.) (1964) *Truth*, Prentice Hall.

PITKIN, H.F. (1972) *Wittgenstein and Justice*, Berkeley, University of California Press.

POLANYI, M. (1958) *Personal Knowledge*, RKP.

POPHAM, W.J. (1967) *Educational Criterion Measures*, Inglewood California, Southwest Regional Laboratory for Educational Research and Development.

POPKEWITZ, T.S. (1984) *Paradigm and Ideology in Educational Research*, Lewes, Falmer Press.

POPKEWITZ, T.S. (Ed.) (1987) *Critical Studies in Teacher Education*, Lewes, Falmer Press.

POPPER, K.R. (1945) *The Open Society and its Enemies*, in 2 vols, RKP.

POPPER, K.R. (1961) *The Poverty of Historicism*, RKP.

POPPER, K.R. (1963) *Conjectures and Refutations*, RKP.

POPPER, K.R. (1968) *The Logic of Scientific Discovery*, Hutchinson.

POPPER, K.R. (1972) *Objective Knowledge*, Oxford, Clarendon.

POPPER, K.R. (1976) *Unended Quest*, Fontana.

PRING, R. (1970) 'Philosophy of education and educational practice', *PESGB*, 4.

PRING, R. (1971) 'Bloom's taxonomy: A philosophical critique (2)', *Cambridge Journal of Education*, 2, pp. 83–91.

PRING, R. (1976) *Knowledge and Schooling*, Open Books.

PUTNAM, H. (1971) *Philosophy of Logic*, Allen and Unwin.

PUTNAM, H. (1975) *Mind, Language and Reality: Philosophical Papers vol. 2*, Cambridge University Press.

PUTNAM, H. (1978) *Meaning and the Moral Sciences*, RKP.

PUTNAM, H. (1981) *Reason Truth and History*, Cambridge University Press.

QUINE, W.V.O. (1953) *From a Logical Point of View*, New York, Harper and Row.

QUINE, W.V.O. (1960) *Word and Object*, Cambridge, M.I.T. Press.

QUINE, W.V.O. (1969) *Ontological Relativity and Other Essays*, New York, Columbia University Press.

QUINE, W.V.O. (1970) *Philosophy of Logic*, Prentice Hall.

QUINE, W.V.O. (1974) *The Roots of Reference*, La Salle, Open Court.

QUINE, W.V.O. (1977) 'Facts of the matter', in SHAHAN, R.W. and MERRILL, K.R. (Eds) *American Philosophy: From Edwards to Quine*, Norman, University of Oklahoma Press. Cited as reprinted in SHAHAN, R.W and SWOYER, C. (Eds) (1979) *Essays on the Philosophy of W.V. Quine*, Brighton, Harvester.

QUINE, W.V.O. (1979) 'Cognitive meaning', *The Monist*, 62, 2, pp. 129–42.

REID, L.A. (1969) *Meaning and the Arts*, London, Allen and Unwin.

REID, L.A. (1986) *Ways of Understanding and Education*, Heinemann.

RIZVI, F. (1983) The Fact-Value Distinction and the Logic of Educational Theory, PhD thesis, University of London, King's College.

ROCHE, M. (1973) *Phenomenology, Language and the Social Sciences*, RKP.

ROMANOS, G.D. (1983) *Quine and Analytic Philosophy*, Cambridge, Mass., M.I.T. Press.

RORTY, R. (1980) *Philosophy and the Mirror of Nature*, Oxford, Blackwell.

RORTY, R. (1982) *Consequences of Pragmatism*, Brighton, Harvester.

RYLE, G. (1966) *The Concept of Mind*, Penguin.

SCHEFFLER, I. (1973) *Reason and Teaching*, RKP.

SCHENCK, J.R. (1978) An Analysis of the Concepts of Curriculum through Wittgenstein's concept of Language Games, PhD thesis, Washington State University.

SCHLEIERMACHER, F. (Ed.) (1977) *Hermeneutics: the Handwritten Manuscripts*, Kimmerle H. Scholars Press, Missoula, Montana.

SELLARS, W. (1963) *Science Perception and Reality*, RKP.

SHACKLE, G.L.S. (1979) *Imagination and the Nature of Choice*, Edinburgh University Press.

SIMON, B. and WILLCOCKS, J. (Eds) (1981) *Research and Practice in the Primary Classroom*, RKP.

SNOOK, I.A. (Ed.) (1972) *Concepts of Indoctrination*, RKP.

STENHOUSE, L. (1975) *An Introduction to Curriculum Development*, Heinemann.

STRAWSON, P.F. (1970) *Meaning and Truth*, Oxford, Clarendon.

TARSKI, A. (1944) 'The semantic conception of truth', *Philosophy and Phenomenological Research*, 4.

TAYLOR, C. (1985) *Philosophical Papers*, in 2 vols, Cambridge University Press.

THOMPSON, J.B. (1981) *Critical Hermeneutics*, Cambridge University Press.

THOMPSON, J.B. and HELD, D. (Eds) (1982) *Habermas: Critical Debates*, Cambridge, M.I.T. Press.

TIBBLE, J.W. (Ed.) (1966) *The Study of Education*, RKP.

TUDOR, A. (1982) *Beyond Empiricism*, RKP.

TYLER, R. (1950) *Basic Principles of Curriculum and Instruction*, University of Chicago Press.

VINCENT, B. and VINCENT, T. (1985) *Information Technology and Further Education*, Kogan Page.

WALKER, J.C. (1984) 'Dusting off educational studies: A methodology for implementing certain proposals of John Wilson's', *JPE*, 18,1.

WARNOCK, M. (1977) *Schools of Thought*, Faber.

WARNOCK, M. (1979) *Education: A Way Ahead*, Oxford, Blackwell.

WARNOCK, M. 'Teacher teach thyself', The 1985 Richard Dimbleby Lecture, printed in *The Listener*, 28 March 1985, pp. 10–14.

WARNOCK, M. (1989) *A Common Policy for Education*, Oxford, Oxford University Press.

WHITE, D.J. (1969) *Decision Theory*, Allen and Unwin.

WHITE, J. (1982) *The Aims of Education Restated*, RKP.

WHITE, J. and WHITE, P. (1986) 'Education, liberalism and human good', in COOPER, D.E. (Ed.) *Education, Values and Mind: Essays for R.S. Peters*, pp. 142–79, RKP.

WILSON, B.R. (Ed.) (1970) *Rationality*, Oxford, Blackwell.

WILSON, J. (1972) *Philosophy and Educational Research*, Slough, NFER.

WILSON, J. (1975) *Educational Theory and the Preparation of Teachers*, Slough, NFER.

WILSON, J. (1982) 'The credibility of educational studies', *Oxford Review of Education*, 8, pp. 3–19.

WINCH, P. (1958) *The Idea of a Social Science and its Relation to Philosophy*, RKP.

WINCH, P. (1972) *Ethics and Action*, RKP.

WITTGENSTEIN, L. (1953) *Philosophical Investigations*, Oxford, Blackwell.

WITTGENSTEIN, L. (1958) *Preliminary Studies for the 'Philosophical Investigations': The Blue and Brown Books*, Oxford, Blackwell.

WITTGENSTEIN, L. (1961) *Tractatus Logico-Philosophicus*, RKP.

WITTGENSTEIN, L. (1969) *On Certainty*, Oxford, Blackwell.

WITTGENSTEIN, L. (1977) *Culture and Value*, Oxford, Blackwell.

WITTGENSTEIN, L. (1979) *Wittgenstein and the Vienna Circle: Conversations recorded by Friedrich Waismann*, Oxford, Blackwell.

WOLFF, J. (1975) *Hermeneutic Philosophy and the Sociology of Art*, RKP.

WRINGE, C. (1988) *Understanding Educational Aims*, Unwin Hyman.

Index

Index

Peters R.S. 20
phenomenalism 25
philosophy
  and educational theory 158
  of education 157
piecemeal social engineering 84
pluralism 88
policy 7
  guiding practice 31, 54
  isolation from theory and practice
    24
  making 132, 134
  self-referential 54
political education 133
Popper K. 58, 60, 84, 121
  and problem solving 89
pornography 156
post-empiricist philosophy of science
  59
practical 11
  discourse 157
  discursive conception of rationality
    127, 146, 147, 148, 155, 157
  interest 96
  judgment 87, 157
  knowledge 38, 79, 86, 152
pragmatism 7, 10, 36, 75, 80
praxis 6
prejudice 39, 80, 101
privatization 44
professional practice 83
professional studies 160
professionalism 50
promotion 52
psychology 160
Putnam H. 81, 93
  and cluster theory of reference 93
  and linguistic division of labour 93
  and principle of charity 93

Quine W.V.O. 7, 58, 59, 65, 70
  and indeterminacy of radical
    translation 66, 81
  and language learning 69
  and ontological relativity 67

rationalism 8, 25, 29
rationality 8, 24, 79, 134, 152
  discursive 121

means-ends 18
of primitive societies 91
practical discursive and systems
  theoretic 122
trans-cultural 92
reason 83
reflection 107, 120
relativism 8, 9, 55, 62, 65, 72, 79, 86,
  116, 146
research programmes
  progression and degeneration 63
resources 149
revolutionary science 75, 89
Rizvi F. 18, 31, 85
romanticism 137
Rorty R. 7, 8, 10, 69
  and normal discourse 115
  and sense of community 49
Ryle G. 19

Scheffler I. 25
Schleiermacher F. 107
school experience 159
schools
  and commerce 154
  and examination results 147
  parental support for 147
  private 4, 132, 157
  private versus state 132, 157
science 8, 9
  and technology 133
  experimental and theoretical 131
  natural 14, 27, 36, 58, 74, 79, 88,
    92
  natural and social 96, 98
  social 36
scientific discovery 62
scientific method 69
seamless web 68, 74, 96
self-interest 44
Sellars W. 74
semantics 66
skills
  life, social etc. 40
solidarity 11, 145
stability in educational discourse 132
student-centred 54, 153
system of belief 25
systematic virtue 68, 71

R